Akshaya Bahibala is a bookseller, poet, publisher and library activist. He is the co-founder of Walking BookFairs, an independent bookstore and publishing house and one of the country's most popular bookmobiles that has travelled more than 35,000 kilometres across 20 states to spread the love of reading. Akshaya has written four books in Odia. This is his first book in English. When he isn't travelling across India, he lives in Bhubaneswar with his partner Satabdi and friend Malu and their cats.

BHANG JOURNEYS

Stories, Histories, Trips and Travels

Akshaya Bahibala

SPEAKING TIGER

SPEAKING TIGER BOOKS LLP
125A, Ground Floor, Shahpur Jat, near Asiad Village,
New Delhi 110049

ISBN: 978-93-5447-986-1
eISBN: 978-93-5447-857-4

10 9 8 7 6 5 4 3 2 1

Typeset in Goudy Old Style by SÜRYA, New Delhi
Printed at HT Media Ltd, Greater Noida

Smoke kills and sometimes heals.
I was stoned for years and then came madness.
I am thankful to lovers, friends and family–
who were sometimes the reason for the madness,
and sometimes, the cure.

Puri–Nov 13, 1962

Pot tricks–peter blows nose & I think it's matches burning in his face. In the teashop off the beach...

Sunset, sitting cross-legged on the sand bank overlooking the ocean below, waves roar like car crashes–in the blue spread orange circle inching below the horizon, green waters, facing my eye, in my head [...]

Can't write much despite the brilliance of the small temples–too much Ganja–I can't keep track of my thoughts without effort. What was the fourth thought back? Struggled over that for a day, like remembering dreams...

– Allen Ginsberg, *Indian Journals*

CONTENTS

My Days with Bhang and Ganja

Beach Road Memories, 1998-2008

Inside a small police outpost—a *phandi*, as we call it—on Beach Road. I'm drinking a cold beer with a friend while a police constable is preparing a chillum and assuring us that no motherfucker can mess with us. 'Let's have some more beer,' he suggests. 'Give me two-three hundred more. Let's buy more beer.'

He's the police. Who am I to argue?

Ten years go by like this. You wake up. You roll a joint. You smoke it. You go to the beach. You meet a bunch of friends, old friends, joint friends, and sometimes a few hippies, White folk. You roll some more joints. Or fill and fire some chillums. You drink some beer or swig Old Monk rum and hang out at the beach or under a banyan tree and you smoke. Rinse. Repeat.

One day you look at a calendar by mistake. You realize you have lost a lot of years smoking and rolling, smoking and rolling.

You meet a woman who loves to smoke and talk and sunbathe on the beach and hang out with young men. She might fuck one of them or fall in love with one of them. Her thing. Your thing is bhang. Your thing is ganja.

Bhang. Ganja. Drifting. You are not alone:

A Japanese woman who loves Indian men ends up getting married to a local fisherman. Both are high on ganja. There are worse reasons to get married.

Another Japanese, a man, so stoned on bhang and ganja that his eyes droop and drop as he says how good everything is, how good. The same Japanese man next morning: his eyes drip with tears. Someone from that all-good group on the all-good night stole all his money.

A big British biker. Rolls in slow. At the beginning of his trip to Puri, he smokes ganja rolled with British Swan tobacco. Six months later, he's running out of money and smoking ganja in beedis. He must go. But he plans to come back. He will go to his sunless island and work as a security guard for some months somewhere to make enough to come back to Puri for six months again. He could live his life like this.

Another White guy, a paedophile. He likes his boys young. He gives them ganja, gets them stoned, hosts drinking parties for them. He comes to Puri every year, until one day some other guy is arrested for seducing a minor and it is no longer safe.

A German guy. Scene 1: In only his underwear, he cleans the railway tracks in the hot afternoon near the railway crossing on the way to the beach because he is madly in love with an Indian woman, she'll come this way, he wants to marry her. Scene 2: This same German guy cleans his hotel room with water and disinfectant in the middle of the night because it is dirty. Scene 3: He smokes up and plays the violin into the early hours of the morning.

A man asks you whether you would like to eat in an expensive restaurant. He's Italian and gay and you smoke and drink together. You can see he hopes to get you into bed. You smoke. You drink. You disappear. The Italian does not ask you out again, but his smile when he sees you is forgiving.

A French woman drinks bhang for meditation and smokes ganja for slimming. She's high one day and wants to make out on the beach. A young man is happy to oblige. They get down to it when a pack of young men arrive and surround them. They scare the shit out of the woman and she runs away half-naked. The pack now begin to kick the shit out of the young man. How dare he get lucky? How dare he soil our great Indian culture?

An Israeli woman smokes only big chillums. With 20 men staring. She makes their dicks shrink. She cleans the chillum like a pro and makes water bongs in the middle of the night with Coca-Cola PET bottles, chocolate wrappers and hollow papaya stems.

A Swiss woman high on ganja fucks two men. There's a third man in the room, he's making a record of all of this. He then blackmails her with her sex video.

A Russian woman calls you Krishna and feeds you prasad from the temple and gives you a 50-rupee note as dakshina. You are both stoned.

The Italian Krishna lover, Maya. She sang love songs to Krishna and kept smoking ganja until she went mad and had to be taken away for rehab.

Ricky. Young, Austrian, an engineer. He loves to smoke up and to drink up. Falls in love with a woman who sells vegetables, marries her and has a child with her and tries to open a small café which is pulled down by the local mafia.

Cut to the same Austrian, Ricky, still young, one-time engineer, dying on the road without medical attention, burned in some unknown place by the local police. When his family come looking for their son, there are ashes in a battered urn.

You remember him, Ricky. He was a genius with computers and probably the one who helped set up the first internet café on Beach Road. Those days, the internet connections were very slow, they were called dial-up connections. Puri had no computer stores, no office had a computer, everything was run manually.

You remember: Ricky and another British guy talking about how computers and the internet would change the world in the next few years, and you, nodding without understanding any of it. But they were your first computer teachers. You have something to thank him for, young Ricky.

He wasn't the only one to die on a lonely road. There were so many, or so you heard. Some you knew. That Swiss woman who loved her ganja and her bhang went out for a walk and dropped dead in the middle of the night. She was cremated, too, according to Hindu rites. Her family never got to know. The embassy never got to know. She was, and then she wasn't.

~

As ten years slipped through my fingers like sand on Beach Road, Puri, I kept an occasional notebook. These fragments are from that handwritten notebook. The Beach Road area was frequented back then by the last of the hippies and the early backpackers. One lot dropping out, the other dropping in. The road became very crowded after the invention of the internet—people were logging in, dropping out and dropping in at the same time. Suddenly, there were voyeurs–the tourists who would never take the risk to live, to let go. The kind who wouldn't let even a year slip through their fingers like sand. About that lot, I have nothing to say. In any case, I had moved on by then.

The Pilgrim's Progress

I was in middle school or maybe in high school, around thirteen years old, sometime in 1992-93. A friend and I bunked school and came to Beach Road for the first time. The road was some distance away from our street and no one went there except the hippies. We had seen them from a distance, White bodies, half naked, lying in the sun. It was inevitable that we would go there to take a closer look, my friend and I.

There were two young women sleeping on the beach. They were topless. I remember one of them had very erect nipples pointing towards the sky. It was my first encounter with a woman's naked body. After that, I kept coming back to the beach as a school kid to meet these 'foreigners' and collect postage stamps and coins. I had learned a little English in school, and I managed to talk to them somehow. I realized that some of them spoke an English as bad as mine. I discovered that there are so many other languages in the world. Their languages fascinated me. Their naked bodies fascinated me. I had to keep coming back. It drew me, Beach Road, and I liked being drawn to it. I was a pilgrim.

After I finished school in 1996, I left Puri and the beach and went away to attend college for a few years. But the beach kept calling me. I would come back to Beach Road after my exams and meet people, sit down and talk to people. This is where I learned to smoke and drink.

The hippies were my inspiration. They gave me the strength to quit my graduation halfway and take off on my own; to do what *I* wanted to do in life; to be free. I did not know then that their world was very different from mine. What would I have done if I had known? I don't know. I might have buckled down and done what everyone else wanted me to do. Ignorance is sometimes bliss.

And so, in 1999, I ran away to Goa. I had heard about Goa on the beach in Puri. I only needed to get to Goa, I thought, just wander around on the beaches, and freedom would find me. Things didn't turn out that way. I worked as a receptionist and a waiter in various hotels and restaurants. I didn't know that the pay would be shit and that you would get treated very badly by your employer and by the guests as well.

I came back to my birth town Puri as if my education was yet to be completed. The beach was my university.

One of the greatest institutions on Beach Road was the Government Bhang Shop. Every foreigner who came to the hippie beach of Puri would visit this institution. It was as if the Government Bhang Shop was a library and you had to go there every day to learn new things and read new stories. Everyone came to the Government Bhang Shop. The tourists, the touts, the louts, the hangabouts, they all came to the Bhang Shop.

So did I.

Welcome to the Government Bhang Shop. You put your hand through a small hole in the shopfront made of crisscrossed wooden planks. You hand over a fifty-rupee note, ask for one tola of ganja. The guy behind the planks wraps it in old newspaper and hands it over to you. If you know the guy well, he will open the little door to the bhang shop and you go and sit with him, have a few chillums, and take your time selecting the best buds and come out happy.

The shop sold bhang—the dry leaves of the cannabis plant—which is legal. It also sold ganja—the dry buds and flowers of the cannabis plant—which is illegal. Bhang is generally had as a drink—as a lassi or thandai—or as a paste rolled into a little ball. Ganja is smoked—in chillums, bidis, cigarettes.

The small police outpost near the Government Bhang Shop never bothers the guy behind the counter who sells illegal ganja. Many police constables have smoked ganja with me on the road, as they've done with many others. Some of the constables will complain about not getting good ganja and then happily share what you've been smoking and say, 'I know you always have good stuff on you.' Sometimes, they even ask you if you've got a piece of charas. Now that is hard stuff. I tried that too. But pulled away in time. Some instinct for self-preservation, I suppose.

My thing was ganja.

I started in easy.

First, a chillum or a joint once or twice a day. You feel light and happy at first, forget all worries. Slowly, the euphoria becomes a habit. You start living in a little world of your own, weightless, filled only with sweet-smoke.

Then you graduate to a tola, around ten grams, of ganja from the Government Bhang Shop once a week.

Then a tola of ganja once a day.

Then a tola in the morning and a tola in the evening.

The routine: Wake up. Have a joint. Take a shower. Walk to Beach Road or take a ride on your bike to the Government Bhang Shop. Buy a tola for Rs 50. Roll a joint in front of the Bhang Shop. One with Shiva in an auto rickshaw, one with Bulu standing on the roadside next to the tea stall, one with Jimmy-the-foreigner in the shade of a beach shack made of palm leaves, one with Sipu under the banyan tree on the veranda of the Trinath temple at sunset. Get thirsty. Have a cup of tea, a glass of water, sometimes a small packet of biscuits or a piece of cake. A small meal here and there. Another joint with some French woman, and one with a Japanese guy in the evening in a restaurant, always the same restaurant. A few rounds of chillum with some Israeli tourist till late in the night. Nicely stoned, return to room. Make one more joint. Go to sleep on a mattress on the floor. Everything often paid for by the tourists, just like that, no services rendered. Sometimes, you beg money from friends and family to buy ganja and drinks.

Another day begins: Late morning, back to Beach Road. Listen to Bob Marley in a restaurant, sitting at a table with some hippies. Share bhang biscuits and sing along: 'No woman, no cry.' All stoned.

~

I am not going to take days and months telling you all the stories of each day and night I spent on that

Beach Road. Let me give you just two of the incidents, the other stories I will save for another day.

Ganja, Magic Mushrooms, Prison

Somewhere around 2007. I'm smoking, sitting around on Beach Road doing nothing, as I have for years. The ganja has already started playing tricks on my mind and out of nowhere an urgent thought comes to me that I must leave Beach Road. I must.

I get up and begin to beg the people I'm with on the beach for some money. Over the next couple of days, I keep doing this—borrowing money from foreigners I know, from friends, even from close relatives, telling them that I want to work and quit all this smoking and drinking shit. I take a train. I head to South India. I travel around South India. I don't remember much, except one image from Hampi on a ganja afternoon: the hills and the riverbank filled with foreigners and the temple ruins and a restaurant under a big mango tree, and a sun-drenched temple on top of a hill, and a big banana plantation on the river bank—all shimmering, hazy. Sometimes I consider looking for a job and sticking to it, and then I tell myself not to bother. It's easier meeting tourists and getting stoned and doing nothing. I will travel, I think, I will go away with them to their country where I have heard things are better...

After a week or so of travelling stoned, I ended up in Kodaikanal with the last of the money I had. I had already decided to go back to my Beach Road in Puri and to my father's house and the Government Bhang Shop and the easy life of not doing anything, but before that I wanted to have a look around Kodaikanal.

A local auto driver took me around and showed me the lake in the middle of the town, the Suicide Point on the hilltop called Dolphin Nose, the pine forest, and then he talked about magic mushrooms.

Already high on ganja, I spent the last of my money buying almost a kilogram of magic mushrooms to take back to my Beach Road friends as a gift.

Later in the evening I had a huge portion of the magic mushrooms in an omelette and smoked ganja again and drank cheap black rum.

The magic mushroom, ganja and rum together made me so high that I was looking for stars on the rooftop of the little lodge on the cold, cold night of Kodaikanal. I couldn't sleep the whole night. In the morning, I realized that I didn't have enough money, so I sold the ivory pendant my mother's elder sister had given me. My aunt's father-in-law had given her the piece of ivory; it was a piece of the ivory from the handle of his ganja-cutting knife.

Then I bought my ticket home from Kodai.

Two days later I was back on my beloved Beach Road and the Government Bhang Shop. The same evening, I gave my magic mushroom gift to my friends.

We gathered at a local restaurant run by a friend, Sameer. We cleaned the shrooms, which had been wrapped in a piece of old newspaper. Then Sameer chopped them up to make omelettes with them. He said he'd add a dollop of bhang as well and laughed. We helped him, smoking ganja and listening to Pink Floyd.

When the shroom omelettes were almost ready, another friend, Jameer, came into the restaurant along with a young British guy who was visiting Beach Road for the first time and was also travelling out of his country alone for the first time.

Jameer introduced us as the group who always loved to have fun.

'They are the ones to look for if you need drugs,' he said, pointing at our chillum and ganja stash.

Jameer and the British guy sat at a table next to us and we shared our ganja and magic shroomlettes with them. We left the restaurant late in the night. Next morning, I went to meet my mother who lived in a nearby village and spent a few days there.

When I came back to Beach Road, I was told that Sameer and Jameer had been badly beaten up by the man who owned the hotel where the British guy had been staying. He had sent his goons to beat them, accusing them of having given the British guy hard drugs. Now both were in prison, based on the FIR registered by the Briton.

Soon, the word on the street was that the police might arrest me too if they found me on Beach Road.

The next day, some friends and I arranged a meeting with Sameer and Jameer in prison. Jameer was scared and crying. He asked for help and begged us to get him out on bail somehow. We bribed a prison guard to take Sameer the ganja I had brought for him and some food for both.

Meanwhile, the British guy had left town. Nobody ever saw him again. He had vanished. Maybe he went back to England, or flew to another exotic destination where he'd find some other poor fuckers to take the blame for his own fumbling adventures.

Sameer and Jameer had to stay in the prison for more than a month before they got bail.

Through all this, it was business as usual on Beach Road, whose denizens kept finding their drug of choice in the Government Bhang Shop just as easily as before.

The Binayak Club Boys Come Hunting

I wake up in my father's house in Puri to the sound of people shouting outside. They sound like young men, late teens or early twenties.

'Motherfucker, come out! We're going to kill you today.'

I had been out till very late and had only a groggy memory of the night before.

'Come out, bastard, and see what we'll do to you!'

Discretion being the better part of valour, I slipped out of the house and went next door to my aunt's place. This was my mother's elder sister. I hunkered down in one of her rooms.

Outside: 'Coward, bastard, come out, and we'll cut your balls off and stick them up your nose.'

Someone from the neighbourhood came into my aunt's house, looking for me. He was excited, he was terrified, he was curious.

'What have you done? The Binayak Club guys are outside. With swords, knives, sticks! One even has a gun.'

In my state, his face looked enormous, filling my vision.

'Don't go out, do you hear me? Just run away from here. They've come to kill you. Run away or they will kill you. Don't think they won't. They killed that young fellow like you a few months ago. And the betel-shop guy? Remember how he struggled for his life for months in a hospital after their attack? He can't talk properly even now. No one can do anything to help you here, everyone fears them. Just go away.'

Outside, the noise grew louder.

'Come on, motherfucker, show your face! We're ready for you. You won't get away today.'

I was shivering with fear. All I wanted was a joint, but I had nothing with me. Even if I'd had some left over, I couldn't smoke inside my aunt's house, and I couldn't step out. Without a smoke, I couldn't put my mind together.

For one mad moment, I thought of calling the police, but I knew the local check post wouldn't respond to my calls. They might even arrest me for what I now remembered I had done the night before together with my friend Sipu.

And so, I crouched like a frightened animal in a corner of the room I was in. Paralyzed with fear but for the violent trembling.

Do you blame me? Binayak Club on my street is for men only. Men go there to become men. They exercise, they want to become bodybuilders. Some sit around all day long, playing cards and carom and swearing. They drink in the evening, smoke ganja and organize a cultural event once a year where they invite music bands and girls to perform famous Bollywood item songs. They organize a Ganesh puja once a year around Ganesh Chaturthi and during the elections they campaign for whichever political party will give them good money. They feast almost every night and keep their aspidistras flying by keeping the women at bay. No girls.

They raise funds in the usual manner. They run a protection racket. They keep the shopkeepers in the area safe from themselves in return for a fee. If anyone protests, the musclemen put down their barbells, spit on their hands and get to work. They boast they can break every single bone in your body in a matter of minutes. They take a cut on each land or house sale. They have been known to stop trucks carrying bricks and unload a few bricks each time they pass through the street as 'a donation'.

You are either with the Binayak Club or you are the enemy. I was not a member of the club nor had I ever participated in any of their activities, not even for a drink of bhang on festive occasions. I didn't know it then, but the leader of the Binayak Club had had an eye on my father's property for a long time. I was the last obstacle between my father's house and him. All this I found out some years later when this man scared off and chased away prospective buyers and forced my family to sell the house to him for half its market value.

But back to the night before the day the Binayak Club Boys came calling. I was with my friend Sipu. He was not from our street but came there often, which the Binayak Club boys didn't like. Sipu and I were heading to my father's house that night when someone shouted something from the Binayak Club. I was too stoned and can't recall what triggered the fight, but I remember Sipu responding to the shouting from the Binayak Club. He roared, 'Motherfucker!' Sipu was big and difficult to handle. A fight broke out between the Binayak Club leader and Sipu. Other Binayak Club boys came running and stopped the fight and we went to my father's house. That might have been the end of it but one more joint on the roof and Sipu got high again and went back to the Binayak Club with a big stick in his hand, looking for the club leader. Sipu broke all the decorative lights and the signboard of the Binayak Club and smashed the glass windows. He came back and we went to sleep on the roof terrace. The next morning Sipu woke up early and left and I went back to sleep. Then came the shouting:

'Where are you, motherfucker? Come here! We are going to fuck you a new hole today, then cut you into pieces and throw you into the Bay of Bengal.'

All morning, I hid in that room in my aunt's house, trembling, till the Binayak Club boys got tired and left, saying, 'We'll be back, motherfucker. This isn't over.'

I ran away from Puri that afternoon.

Recovery

After running away from Puri, I had no option but to get a job to survive. Until then, I didn't know how taking bhang and ganja daily for some years had affected my body and mind and how difficult it would be for me to get back to regular life. Living in a constant high from cannabis, I had lost connection with the real world, which demanded a lot more from me than just smoking, drinking and hanging out with tourists.

So I came to Bhubaneswar and was staying with friends while I tried to clean up and get back into the real world. I was clean of any substance for almost six months. Then Maha Shivratri 2008 rolled around, and my friends said I could do some ganja because I would be smoking in the name of Lord Shiva. I smoked a huge bucket bong with a few friends on the roof.

I was back. I was where I knew the scene. Or so I thought.

For two or three rounds of the bong, I was just talking with friends. But then came madness and a consuming fear, erupting from somewhere, I don't know where. The sound of the temple prayer kept ringing in my ears, and I just couldn't move from the place. I sat on the roof for a long time, terrified. I felt that everyone was going to come and attack me or kill me. I didn't want to go down with my friends and have dinner. I asked everyone to just leave me alone and go.

I sat on the roof till midnight. My past kept flashing in front of my eyes. With great effort of will, I finally managed to go down to my room on the first floor. I bolted the door, took a blanket and hid myself under it and tried to sleep.

I woke up the next day and decided to stop smoking ganja. I realized that my mind was playing tricks on me. The abrupt return to ganja had triggered something and put me in the grip of paranoia.

I tried, I slipped. Tried. Slipped.

I remember one time when I slipped. A spring morning. It was Holi and I went out in a car with three of my friends to play and party. We rolled down the windows and let the breeze flow in. One of my friends had brought bhang laddoos along. I tried a laddoo and liked the taste of it. Then I kept eating the laddoos, one after the other, and eventually, I lost count of how many I had eaten.

We splashed each other with water, with colour. We laughed at our faces and our hair. We laughed at other people. In the afternoon, we stopped to have a lassi along the way. While waiting for the lassi at the bhang shop, the bhang in the laddoos started kicking in. We had our lassi and came out. It was the same world as when we went in: the same Holi, the same colours, the same people laughing and splashing and smearing each other with handfuls of colour. But it was also not the same. Suddenly, everything was scary, and I was gripped by a feeling of extreme fear. There was something menacing about the crowd of people, there was something eerie about the colours. The fear grew, I ran out and got into the car.

I tried telling myself that this was only cannabinoids binding with the receptors of my brain and triggering my amygdala. The words came through, the science and the knowledge were there, but they were overwritten by the fear.

I tried to pull myself away from my fear, I tried to breathe deep, but the dread, the feeling of the terrifying strangeness-in-the-ordinary persisted. The highways were empty but for a few motorbikes and their sound was unnaturally amplified, and all else silent, dead: Zombie Apocalypse. Now I began to feel as if I were in a bad horror movie, and suddenly the people on the motorbikes were drenched in blood, they were Life-in-Death and Death-in-Life. The movie was the only reality, and I was trapped in it. This movie would not end.

I looked over at my friend who was driving, and I began to think: Oh no, oh God, no, she's been shot too, and she's driving, she's covered in blood and she's driving. Then she turned to look at me, blank, blood-soaked, and I guessed that she had discovered she was also in this never-ending movie. I tried to keep her out of the script by looking out of the window at the empty highway and tried to remember how this movie would end, tried not to think about someone falling onto the windscreen suddenly or running alongside the car, wet with blood and intent on...on doing what? Terror, that was all I knew.

Somehow, we managed to come back home, I went into the shower and stayed in the shower for an eternity. I don't remember how and when I came out of the shower.

Later, my friends and family said that I had slept for more than a day, didn't wake up even once and didn't eat anything.

This is how I made a movie, co-directed by bhang.

~

The road to recovery wasn't easy. Simply deciding to quit drugs didn't cure me overnight of low confidence and an almost paralyzing fear of everything around me. Incapable of any social contact outside a small, tight circle, with great difficulty I managed to get a job at a computer hardware store for Rs 200 a day. After some time, I got into Vodafone, selling SIM cards for Rs 5,500 a month; then moved to a bookstore and sold books for few years, before starting my own bookstore with my partner.

I have been on firm ground for 15 years now. Recently, on our way back to Bhubaneswar from Puri with friends, we stopped at a tea stall to have a cup of tea. The place was filled with ganja smoke. I asked the teashop owner about it and he showed me a nice pack of crisp pre-rolled joints. How much the world had changed. We started talking about bhang and ganja, about how it used to be when I was a slave to both. It wasn't all bad, now that I had come through that long, sapping phase, I said. I had memories, I began to talk about them, and Ravi Singh, my publisher and friend, said: 'Why don't you put these in a book?'

I went back to my old notebook. And I went around Odisha, collecting other stories.

What a world it was. What a world it is...

A Bhang-Ganja Journal

The Government Bhang Shop Brahmin

Sir, I am a brahmin bhang shop owner. My father was a very reputed brahmin of good social standing. Here, take a look at this photo, my father is with ministers and social workers. Big people. I don't do anything wrong, sir. I just sell pure bhang drink, I don't mix it with any rubbish that might make it poisonous. If you try my bhang drink you will be fit, sir. It's natural, an ayurvedic herb, it's good for health.

Sir, bhang has been in our culture for thousands of years. Who knows the exact time? It has always been legal. I don't do anything illegal. Sorry, sir, the signboard saying this is a government-licensed bhang shop was blown away in the last storm. Please give me some time. I will put it up again very soon. I know the law says it is mandatory to have that sign. Trust me, I have already asked the painter to make a new one. It will be up on the shop before your next visit.

Our bhang shop is one of the oldest in town, more

than 40 years old. My father started it and now I take forward his legacy. We don't make a lot of money from selling bhang, sir. On a good day, we sell a kilogram of bhang, but very little otherwise. I don't even weigh the bhang I sell, sir, years of making bhang balls has turned my hands in to a weighing machine.

I buy my bhang from the government depot only, sir. No, I won't lie—I also buy some from drug peddlers at a cheaper price, sir. The bhang provided by the government depot is Rs 590 per kilo because of the high excise duty—all the bhang comes from UP, you see. The bhang I buy from the drug peddlers is only Rs 200 per kilo. Also, the bhang that I get from the Government Bhang Gola is always old stock, whereas the drug peddlers give me good-quality, fresh bhang. That is the truth, sir. I am a good brahmin, I won't lie.

I will tell you whatever you ask me...Yes, I know, sir, I should only sell the bhang leaves as per excise law, nothing else, no byproducts. But the demand is high for bhang lassi and if I don't fulfil the demands of the customers then I will lose all the business. Tell me then, how will I feed my family, sir?

But I only sell good bhang lassi, sir, no mixing with any bad products. I can guarantee my bhang is the purest in town. You can send samples from all the bhang-sellers in town to a laboratory and test them, test them and see, mine will be the best quality. This brahmin won't lie or cheat, sir.

The city has more than ten licensed, legal bhang shops but there are hundreds of illegal bhang shops. Ours is the purest bhang shop. After selling around 30 kilos of bhang, I make a small profit of Rs 15,000 or Rs 20,000 a month. Very difficult to manage a family of five with this income, sir. Thank God, we are brahmins and I can make some money doing pooja-paath for marriages and other religious ceremonies. That is how we survive.

You know, sir, sometimes I don't like selling bhang or doing this type of business at all, but what to do? I must do something—five stomachs to fill. This is my son, he also sits in the shop sometimes, but he is a graduate in commerce and going for higher studies. My daughter is studying law. Once both my children get big jobs, I don't have to continue selling bhang. My children will earn more in a day than what I earn in a month.

Many people come to buy bhang to make medicine, sir. Our society and our neighbours consider bhang good. Many women also take bhang from us, they come with their husbands. The women tell us to give their husbands bhang whenever they come, as the women are trying to free their husbands from alcohol addiction. They say after consuming bhang, the husbands become calmer and don't shout in the streets or get into fights.

They become quiet and harmless. The children are also happier now that their father is quiet and there is peace in the family. Sir, I'm telling you—bhang makes people calm and peace-loving, unlike alcohol, which is a menace to society. After consuming bhang, people become believers in non-violence, if someone slaps them on one cheek, they will turn the other cheek. Just like Jesus. I would blame alcohol and politics for all the crimes in our state. Bhang gives people shanti.

Even daughters tell their fathers, 'Papa, don't drink alcohol. Please take bhang.' We even have entire families coming together to buy bhang.

I make many types of bhang sharbat, sir, my cold almond sharbat with saffron and bhang is famous. You must try it.

I never sell bhang to children. Never. If someone sends a child to my shop and the boy says that he is buying for his father, I say, 'Tell your Papa to come.' I don't know the law about the minimum age limit for consuming bhang, but I don't give it to anyone below the age of 20-22. Imagine what would happen if I gave a small dose of bhang to a child—the child might end up at death's door! I have heard of people being hospitalized and put on saline after consuming bhang. It is because they don't know how to handle it. I have heard about regular hard drinkers being unable to digest even fifty-paise-worth of bhang and having to be taken to the hospital ICU. But nothing serious happens to them; after a few hours, they are released from hospital. Sir, I have never heard of anyone dying after consuming bhang as they do after alcohol or other drugs.

I also take a little bit of bhang every day. At least twice, about ten grams. My father also consumed it; I'm continuing the family tradition. Bhang improves your digestion, your stomach is always clean. Your face also starts glowing. But ladies in the house don't drink bhang, sir. I also eat paan like my father, but my son doesn't take anything, sir.

All the bhang shops' quality should be checked in a laboratory at least once a year, sir. People are paying money and they deserve good quality. Other bhang shops are mixing ingredients which are harmful for the human body, but mine is the purest, sir. Other bhang shops say that their bhang gives the best high, but my policy is different. I promise purity. I like my customers to have the best quality so that they can come back to me for more, again and again, eat two bhang golis instead of one, and that way I can sell more. What is the point of mixing harmful ingredients and making customers high with small dosages of bhang?

Do you want to try my bhang, sir? If you have never consumed bhang, then a pea-sized goli is enough to start with. If you consume more than a tiny bhang-paste ball you will see the moon and stars in broad daylight.

Never has a person or a family cursed me for selling bhang, because my bhang has never harmed anyone. Many say bhang has brought peace and happiness in their family, unlike alcohol, which only brought unhappiness and financial difficulties to many. That's why I continue selling bhang.

I sell around one kilo of bhang every day, sir. Many people come looking for ganja but I scold them and tell them to never come back to my shop again. Almost all the other bhang shop owners sell ganja, which is illegal. You can only sell bhang from a government-licensed bhang shop; till some years ago, you could sell some opium under license, and some ganja, then it was stopped. But many shop owners sell ganja illegally. I have never done it, and I won't do it in the future. Ganja is very bad, sir. When ganja was legal and was sold and distributed through the Excise Department before the NDPS [Narcotic Drugs and Psychotropic Substances] Act was implemented in Odisha in 1989, my father was selling it, sir, but we have not sold even a gram of ganja ever since it was declared illegal.

I think around ten to 15 per cent of the people of the city consume bhang, and more and more people are taking it now, but many more are taking alcohol too. But

I think only bhang should be legal; the rest—alcohol and other drugs—should all be banned. Sir, bhang is natural, unlike alcohol and other drugs. Bhang is good, I am doing good work. Why don't you ask Google the benefits of bhang? Many countries in the world have legalized it.

~

The ganja shop owner's point about alcohol being more harmful than ganja is now accepted fact. But this is not what most people will be told. This is not the official or even popular narrative. There are several critics of the ban on ganja that came with the NDPS Act in India, which, among other things, erased the distinction between soft and hard drugs. In Parliament, too, there have been dissenting voices. A former Member of Parliament (MP) from Odisha, Tathagata Satpathy, had criticized the ban on cannabis, or hemp, calling it 'elitist'. Other MPs and activists have been campaigning for legalized, regulated supply of ganja, opium and other non-synthetic intoxicants. This might, they argue, even help bring down the levels of heroin and cocaine addiction in the country.

Procurement and Distribution of Bhang by the Excise Department of Odisha

In 1985, India brought in the Narcotic Drugs and Psychotropic Substances or NDPS Act, which banned the use of the resin, flower and fruit of the cannabis plant. Overnight, ganja became illegal; only bhang, made of the leaves, was legal. The Act was implemented in Odisha in 1989, changing a practice that had been common for millennia. Until 1989, the Excise Department of Odisha supplied both bhang and ganja through its Central Bhang Gola in Cuttack to all licensed sellers. The shops were called Government Ganja Shops then. Before 1989, the Excise Department was even giving licenses to farmers to cultivate cannabis under its supervision in the districts of Sambalpur, Dhenkanal and Cuttack.

The Excise Department of Odisha's Central Bhang Gola in the silver city of Cuttack, the old capital of the state of Odisha, has been in existence since the British

Raj. The Excise Commissioner, Odisha, appoints an Officer in Charge (OIC) at the Central Bhang Gola. This Gola in Cuttack supplies bhang to all the district bhang golas, which further supply to the licensed bhang shops in each district.

Since bhang can no longer be cultivated in Odisha legally, the Excise Department is dependent on Uttar Pradesh, one of the few states where controlled, legal cultivation of cannabis is allowed. In 2019, the Odisha Excise Department made amendments to its excise policy to allow sale of bhang seized in raids to the licensed bhang shops in order to reduce the state's dependency on Uttar Pradesh.

Each district where licensed bhang shops are in operation has a bhang gola in the district headquarters' excise office. Based on the requisition of each district bhang gola, the Central Bhang Gola in Cuttack sources the required amount of bhang from Uttar Pradesh. An officer from the Excise Department, Odisha, travels to Uttar Pradesh to bring it. This amount is then distributed to the district golas and from there to the licensed shops.

Each bhang shop license holder has been issued a username and a password by the Excise Department to log in to the eAbkari portal and generate a challan to purchase the required quantity of bhang. They can pay by debit/credit cards or net banking. They pay the price of the bhang, plus the excise duty, which has been fixed at Rs 500 per kilogram.

Once the challan has been created, the bhang shop owner needs to submit one copy of the challan to the OIC of the district bhang gola who will issue a transport pass, valid for a day or two, for the movement of the bhang to the shop. The OIC will also forward a copy of the challan to the district excise superintendent's office.

After this long, bureaucratic process, bhang reaches the buyer, and at that level it is a simple transaction. Or should be, except that the NDPS Act says that the personal bhang possession limit is fixed at 120 grams, anything above that can be punishable.

~

Two Charts About the Legal Bhang Market in Odisha

The number of bhang shops in Odisha by city/district, as of 2022:

Place	Number of Govt Bhang Shops
Bhadrak	5
Bhubaneswar	8
Khordha	2
Cuttack	28
Jagatsinghpur	11
Kendrapara	10
Puri	35
Brahmapur	1
Ganjam	5
Kandhamal	2
Total	107

Sale of bhang by year:

Year	Bhang sold in licensed shops
2020–2021	5800 kgs
2021–2022	4400 kgs

Bhang in the Nazirkhana

How ancient is the tradition of drinking bhang in Puri, the most fabled of Odisha's cities? Some people say it is as old as the city itself.

How popular is bhang in the city, and how widespread is its consumption? It is difficult to tell. There is little literature available on the subject.

But I remember a conversation with a remarkable person, a retired civil servant, Harihar Panda, which gave me some idea. Memories and impressions are often more useful and revealing than dry facts and data.

Here is an excerpt from Panda's wonderful memoir, *Recollections–Memoirs of a Civil Servant (2022)*, in which he recounts an episode from the 1950s:

> I was surprised to discover in one corner of the office a bare-bodied hefty man engaged in grinding something vigorously without break. The Nazir promptly said, 'This man is a peon of the Nazirkhana who has come

back to the headquarters after spending a fortnight in the remote villages servicing judicial processes on the contesting parties. As there is nothing for him to do in the office, he has been allotted this duty of preparing Bhang.' He hastily went on to add, 'Every day some peons, known as process servers, return to the office after completing their duty in the villages and they have no other work here. Thus, they are assigned this duty to keep them engaged, and this has been the practice since the Britishers' time.'

As I was curious to know all about Bhang, its preparation and utility, the learned Nazir got an opportunity to enlighten me about this precious substance and that perhaps was the best part of my training as a probationer! He spit the crimson betel leaf juice from his mouth into an ugly-looking brass bowl, cleared his throat and continued his lecture: 'The dry leaves of the cannabis plants are famously known as Bhang, whereas their buds, when dry, are called Ganja. The female cannabis plants produce the best Bhang. The transcendental properties of Bhang have been extolled in the *Atharvaveda* as a tool to ward off evil. It is described as a beneficial herb that relieves anxiety.'

[Summing up] his exposition, the Nazir proclaimed Bhang's exalted association with Lord Shiva who, he said, was regarded as the 'Lord of Bhang'...

Emboldened by my helpless innocence the Nazir,

whom I now considered a connoisseur of Bhang, proceeded to describe the expert process of preparing Bhang. 'The dried cannabis leaves are soaked in water for a couple of hours and then they are squashed and ground into a greenish paste...But the grinding has to be done most laboriously for a few hours till the paste acquires a sticky consistency and then only can the Bhang bring about a sense of euphoria in the minds of the users.'

The theory class was over. The Bhang master took me for a practical demonstration, where the peon was engaged in the production process. I examined the [grinding stones] which, barring the size, were the same as those used in an Indian kitchen to grind spices to a paste. But by constant use and certainly with much care and attention, these two tools had acquired a glittering shine. There was no record in the Nazirkhana to show when actually these valuable items were procured, but their existence could be traced to the early days of British rule in Odisha on the basis of the prevalence of Bhang even then. I was surprised to see that the preparation of Bhang had assumed the status of an acknowledged official duty in the Nazirkhana and the Assistant Nazir, known as Naib Nazir, was in charge of supervising the preparation process without the slightest lapse. His method of testing the purity and consistency of Bhang was unique and incredible. He would go, bring the paste to the size of a ball and put it in a mortar. He would then press the pestle on the ball and lift it. Lo! The sticky paste would be lifted up along with the mortar! The test of consistency was thus confirmed and the poor peon was relieved of his onerous duty–of course with a small ball of the precious product he had produced.

It was almost time for the office to close. I was sitting with the Nizarat Officer, Mr. Sahu. The Nazir unexpectedly appeared with something in his hand. I saw a nicely engraved small silver box with a lid which the Nazir humbly produced before his officer. I was appalled to discover that the silver box contained a lump of the Bhang so dexterously prepared after a full day's toil. It was a ritual... Before the close of the office, the Nazir–or the Naib Nazir, in his absence–would start offering the Bhang ceremonially to the officers of the Collectorate, from the Collector downwards according to their rank and status. Mr. Sahu took a small quantity of the seductive substance and gulped it in one swallow. The elderly Nazir humbly invited me to initiate the divine dose which I declined with regret. But I was fascinated by the glittering container. On minute examination I found that the silver box carried an inscription–'WW–1828'. [The date] was evidently the year of its manufacture, and the two letters might possibly stand for William Wilkinson, the first

Collector and District Magistrate of Purusottama, as Puri was called then. It was astonishing that the unique receptacle had retained its glamour and glory during the past one hundred and thirty years...

Twenty-five years passed. I took voluntary retirement from the government service and joined the legal profession. I had gone to Puri several times, but could not visit the Collectorate because of my engagement otherwise. On one occasion, I was attending a land acquisition case in the court of the District Magistrate of Puri. After the hearing was over, the young District Magistrate who was also the Collector of Puri asked me to meet him in his chamber. When I went there, he asked me why I seemed to be visibly absentminded during the court proceedings and if I had any personal problem which he could solve. I narrated my past association with the Collectorate as an officer of the Odisha Administrative Service, which, I confessed, was still lingering in my mind emotionally. The young Collector congratulated me and asked a senior officer to take me round the Collectorate, which was once my seat of activities. The old Collectorate building, which was famously known as the Salt Godown during the early years of the British rule, had been partly demolished and a new wing was constructed to accommodate the important sections of the District Office. I was naturally curious to visit the Nazirkhana where a smart young man had taken charge as the Nazir. The office had assumed an elegant appearance with modern furniture and appliances. But these had no fascination for me, and I asked the Nazir about the practice of preparing Bhang in the Nazirkhana. The Nazir was certainly not prepared for this unexpected query and merely pleaded his total ignorance of such a nefarious activity in a government office. The fond ritual of offering Bhang to the officers had been discontinued as a primitive indulgence. The lovely [grinding-stones] must have been discarded along with the huge debris accumulated during demolition of the old structure, and the one-hundred-and-thirty-year-old pretty silver box might have been stolen–not for its beauty and antiquity, but for the pure silver content. I was dismayed that such a rare object of 1828 AD could not be preserved as memorabilia for posterity to marvel. I returned with moist eyes.

The Master Sharbat Maker

My search for the best bhang lassi makers took me to the master sharbat maker of Puri. I found him in a small lane near the Uttar Kali temple. A fair man in his sixties, in a white dhoti, his torso bare, a gamchha on his shoulder, chewing paan and radiating a very heavy scent of tobacco. He had been making bhang sharbat for the last 25 or 30 years, he said, having learnt the art from his father and forefathers.

'Bhang is not a bad thing,' the master sharbat maker said, 'it is not an addiction. You must know how to consume it. It is to be taken in small quantities to help you digest the food after a good meal and sleep well after a long, hard day's work. Bhang is like medicine for the body, many elderly people use it as medicine. It should only be consumed after sunset. All those stupid people who take it in the daytime to use it as a drug have spoiled the good name of bhang.'

I wondered if I should confess that I had been

stupid, too, for many years. But I had fond memories of Beach Road, and I didn't think he would understand. Besides, I wanted to hear his story, not tell him mine.

'Bhang has been in use for thousands of years,' the sharbat maker continued. 'My grandfather took bhang every day. My mother said her father and grandfather also took bhang every day. I take it too. I don't touch alcohol; it has really corrupted all the youth these days. I don't know why the government is promoting alcohol so much and trying to stop bhang and ganja. The police bothered me so much, I have stopped making and selling bhang lassi. Now I only advertise my famous Chini Sharbat, which you can make with or without bhang. I will be happy to share my recipe with you. But let's have some sharbat first.'

As he made me the sharbat, he said in Hindustani: '*Bhang bhala jo thoda sa khaye; mard bhala jo roj kamaye.*'

Which translates into English as 'Bhang is good if taken in small doses; a man is good if he works and earns every day.'

Then the sharbat maker dictated his recipes.

~

Paanmadhuri Bhang Mishri Sharbat

Ingredients:

Bhang leaves: 50 gm
Sweet fennel seeds: 10 gm
Carom seeds: 10 gm
Black pepper: 10 gm
Rock sugar (Mishri): 100 gm

Method:

- Soak the rock sugar in water and leave overnight. Mix well in the morning.
- Boil the bhang leaves in water for 30 to 40 minutes until the water turns reddish. Drain the water. Wash the bhang leaves again with room-temperature water. Squeeze the water out and then dry the leaves in the sun for a few hours.
- Soak the sweet fennel seeds, black pepper and carom seeds for 30 minutes in water and then mix with the dried bhang leaves and grind everything together to make a paste.
- Mix the thick paste with the rock-sugar syrup and keep in the refrigerator to make a cold and refreshing paanmadhuri bhang mishri sharbat.
- You can also make this drink without bhang if you want to.
- You can store the drink in the refrigerator for a few days and serve it to guests.

Bhang Laddoo

Ingredients:

Bhang leaves 100 gm
Sweet fennel seeds 10 gm
Carom seeds 10 gm
Green cardamom 10 gm
Black pepper 10 gm
Sugar 100 gm
Desi ghee 100 gm

Method:

- Boil the bhang leaves in water for 30 to 40 minutes until the water turns reddish. Drain the water. Rinse the bhang leaves again in room-temperature water. Squeeze the water out and then dry the leaves under the sun.
- Once dried, grind the bhang leaves fine, add sweet fennel seeds, carom seeds, green cardamom, black pepper and grind again. Add sugar as needed and fry the paste in a pan in desi ghee until the sugar becomes sticky.
- Scrape the mixture onto a plate and start shaping into balls with the help of more desi ghee. Allow it to cool. Your bhang laddoos are ready.

Note: The bhang laddoos can be kept in a dry box for months and taken in the evenings to keep your appetite high and bowels clean. The laddoos are delicious but be careful if you are eating them for the first time. One ten-gram bhang laddoo can be enough for two or three grown adults.

Keep out of the reach of children.

~

Pista Badam Kesar Bhang Sharbat

Ingredients:

Bhang leaves 50 gm
Almonds 100 gm
Saffron 10 gm
Rock sugar (Mishri) 100 gm

Method:

- Soak the almonds and the rock sugar overnight, separately.
- Mix the rock-sugar and water thoroughly in the morning to make a syrup.
- Boil the bhang leaves in water for 30 to 40 minutes until the water turns reddish. Drain the water and rinse the bhang leaves in room-temperature water. Squeeze the water out and then dry the leaves under the sun.
- Grind the bhang leaves fine. Then grind the soaked

almonds with saffron and mix with the rock sugar syrup. Keep in the refrigerator to make a cold and refreshing drink.

Note: You can also make this drink without bhang if you just want to have a healthy sharbat without getting high. You can store the drink in the refrigerator for a few days and serve it to guests.

Fifty grams of bhang can be taken by at least 20 to 30 people if they are new to eating bhang. Bhang has very different effects on different people, some keep smiling and are full of joy, some can become just numb, some people can become paranoid, some sleep like a baby, and so on.

Trinath Mela

I was travelling with a team of some 30 men from the police and excise departments tasked with the destruction of illegal ganja plantations in the shimmering greens of Malkangiri and Koraput, South Odisha. I watched as some of the constables plucked a few choice buds of the cannabis plant and tucked them into their backpacks. Soon, they would uproot over 100 acres of the same plant.

'What will you do with those buds?' I asked.

One of them replied: 'These are for a puja to make baba happy.' By baba he meant the god Shiva.

Another constable explained: 'I will give them to the priest and the priest will use some of it to worship Shiva and the rest he will sell. If Shiva is happy then Goddess Parvati will be pleased, and we will have peace and tranquility in our lives.'

Both the constables spoke of the Trinath Mela. The buds they had collected would be useful then.

Every Sunday, almost all the villages and towns in the state of Odisha perform a religious ceremony called Trinath Mela. Trinath means the three chief gods, Brahma, Vishnu and Maheshwara, or Shiva. The Trinath Mela has been a tradition in different parts of the country, including Odisha, for centuries, and ganja figures in the tradition.

Here is one of the many folktales about the origin of the Trinath Mela:

> Once upon a time a brahmin was on his way to the market. He was a bit distracted because his cow had gone missing. He had looked for her everywhere, but she was nowhere to be seen. Now he saw a huge banyan tree ahead, offering a patch of cool shade from the sun. He stopped to enjoy the cool when he heard a voice like a rumble of thunder.
>
> 'Look down, and tell me what you see.'
>
> The brahmin did not know whose voice it was, as there was no one else around; he was quite alone. But he did as he was told and looked down, and saw three coins at his feet, glinting in the sunlight filtering through the banyan leaves.
>
> 'I...I see three one-anna coins,' he stammered.
>
> 'Pick them up,' said the Voice.
>
> 'They do not belong to me,' said the brahmin. 'I cannot take them.'
>
> 'They belong to me,' said the Voice. 'And I give

them to you. Pick them up and go to the market. Buy one anna worth of oil, one anna worth of ganja and one anna worth of paan leaves.'

The brahmin obeyed and picked up the coins. He began to walk to the market again. On the way he met a friend and fell to talking. They finished their shopping and turned to return. The brahmin lost his balance just then and collapsed, and when he tried to get up, he found that he could not. He tried many positions to haul himself up but failed each time. Then suddenly, when he rolled over and was facing the market, he was up on his feet like a shot.

'This is a sign,' his friend said. 'The gods are telling you that you have unfinished business in the market.'

Then the three coins clinked in the fold of the brahmin's dhoti at the waist, and he remembered. He hurried back to the market to get the three things that he had been asked to.

The first two were easy enough, but the third presented a problem.

'Can I have one paise worth of oil?' the brahmin asked the oil-presser.

'Certainly,' said the oil-presser. 'Present your lota.'

'Oh, I didn't bring a lota,' said the brahmin, feeling dashed. Then the Voice sounded in his ear: 'Spread the edge of your dhoti. Trust me.'

The brahmin duly spread the edge of his dhoti and bade the oil-presser to fill it. The oil-seller looked at him incredulously but the brahmin went on standing there, holding out his dhoti. The oil-seller thought the brahmin was simple in the head and saw a chance to make a quick anna. He wiped a can of oil on the edge of the brahmin's dhoti and said, 'There! That's as much as you get for an anna.'

The brahmin made a low bow of thanks and began to walk away. The oil-seller turned around, grinning to himself, and as he did, his elbow knocked over the oil can. The oil began to pour out on the ground. By the time the oil-seller had got the can upright again, only an anna worth of oil was left in it.

He ran after the brahmin and apologized. 'I am sorry. I tried cheat you. Please take your oil.'

The brahmin smiled and spread the edge of his dhoti again. The oil-seller poured the oil in and lo! It stayed there, a small glowing pool of gold in the sun.

Recognizing a miracle, the oil-seller bowed.

The brahmin walked back the way he had come, and when he reached the banyan tree, the Voice spoke: 'Have you brought the offerings?'

'Yes, my Lord,' the brahmin said and was about to set them down when the Voice spoke again: 'You may take these home.'

'But, my Lord, they are yours.'

'What is not mine?' asked the Voice.

The brahmin could not resist asking now: 'May I ask who is speaking?'

'I am Trinath, the Lord of Time. You call me the Maker, the Preserver and the Destroyer. You call me Lord Brahma, Lord Vishnu and Lord Shiva. But I am all three in one and it pleases me for you to call me Trinath. Go home now and sing my praise as you offer these things to the fire which I kindled with an Om at the beginning of human time.'

And so the brahmin went home and lit a fire and began the offering to Trinath. As he added the paan leaves, he heard a low moo. He knew that it was his cow but he went on singing in praise. He added the oil and heard another note. It was the sound of a calf. The cow had given birth in her old age. He added the ganja and suddenly he was very happy and began dancing. A princess passing by saw him dancing and fell in love with his grace and his infectious happiness. She summoned him to her palace and he went with his cow and calf and they lived happily ever after.

~

I decided to participate in the Trinath Mela in my village, which is about 60 kilometres from the state capital, Bhubaneswar. Around 20 families, including ours, live in an extension of the village called Gaudachelli Nuasahi. The forefathers of all these families moved from the overpopulated main village to this patch of barren government land just before Independence and settled there.

They tilled the barren land; they had no choice as they had no money to buy better land, nor access to education that would have led them to other professions. Since then, things have changed and haven't changed. Today, many men from Gaudachelli Nuasahi work as labourers and drivers in towns across Odisha, and even in other states, like Kerala, Goa and Tamil Nadu. The village has a small temple to Lord Shiva and a temple to Trinath. The Trinath temple is a room with a concrete roof, about 30 square feet in area.

The villagers don't know who exactly started the Trinath Mela there, but the elders say it started 20 or 35 years ago under a peepal tree. The present Trinath temple was built some ten years ago. The Trinath Mela is observed every Sunday, and each family contributes by rotation, although a family might ask to be allowed to jump the queue if there is a wish that needs fulfilling.

I decided to do the Trinath Mela on the third Sunday of the month of January 2024, for the success of this book. I reached the village in the afternoon all excited and had chicken curry and saag made on a woodfire and waited for the evening. My elder brother's wife said, 'You must change your clothes before going to the Mela. These clothes are now impure since you ate chicken wearing them.'

Dressed in new clothes, I went to meet the priest at the Trinath temple, who suggested I buy apples, bananas, coconut and chuda (beaten rice) as prasad. I bought these. The main ingredients for the Mela, of course, were paan, oil and ganja–which my mother said Nilu, one of the regular Trinath Mela guys from our neighbourhood, would arrange from the nearby village.

When Nilu came to take the money from my mother for these three main ingredients, I decided to join him on his buying trip. I asked where we would go and he said: 'There are two or three people who sell ganja in the village.'

'Do they sell it only for the puja or can you buy it for your own use?'

'Lots of people smoke it now,' he said. 'Even the Mausa who's going to sell it to us smokes up.' Mausa is a term of respect for older men in Odisha.

'Mausa sells ganja from his home or from a little hut in his fields,' Nilu continued. 'Some people go there to smoke in the evenings.'

After we had bought oil and paan, we went on to

Mausa's house. We knocked on the door of this elder's home a couple of times. A woman was talking on the phone inside, and now we heard her complain: 'I tell you, work, work, work all day, morning to night, and if you just sit down just once to watch five minutes of TV or talk on the phone, someone comes banging on the door.' After we had waited at the door a few minutes, she called out to us, 'Mausa is not home, go to the fields,' and then continued grumbling over the phone.

Off we went, and parked our motorbike on a patch of farmland on the outskirts of the village, and then walked to a small hut. It was dark, and the hut was dimly lit. The roof was so low that I had to bend at the door to see what was inside. The dim light came from a torch propped against something on the mud floor. We saw two men seated on flattened cardboard cartons spread on the floor. In front of them, on a light green polythene sheet, was a heap of tiny newspaper-wrapped packets of ganja. Nilu had told me each little packet cost Rs 20. We asked for two and handed Mausa a fifty-rupee note. He gave us our change and watched without comment as I checked the contents of the packets. Then he and the other, slightly younger, man went back to their ganja packing.

Around seven in the evening, everybody gathered at

the Trinath temple. They sat on the floor of the small concrete veranda. The priest began the preparations for the Mela, while another guy began crushing the ganja I had brought along. A young boy started reading from the Trinath Mela book loudly. I looked inside the tiny temple. There were four stone idols: Brahma, Vishnu, Maheshwara and Ganesha. I walked around for a bit, then went and sat next to the man crushing the ganja.

He put some of the ganja in a clay chillum and started to smoke up. After a couple of long drags, he informed me that the man who played the drums was missing today because a child had been born in his family and he could only join the Trinath Mela after the family had completed the purification ceremony. The man who usually played the cymbals was also missing; he had gone to some other place that was in greater need of the music of the cymbals.

'You must come back another day for the fully fledged Mela when the entire team of musicians is around; it's a spectacle to see.'

The smoke from the chillum made me a bit dizzy. I shifted a little away from the smoker.

Someone asked the boy reading the Trinath Mela book to slow down a bit so that I might also understand.

Someone else from the crowd told me how the

elders of the village had struggled to build this little temple and spent more than Rs 50,000 on the first Mela they organised when the temple was inaugurated. He also asked me to keep coming back to the village and be part of the Mela–and to help improve the temple. 'You will be blessed,' he assured me.

The reading from the Trinath Mela book was completed in around 30 minutes. By that time, the priest had already prepared the prasad. The guy who was smoking ganja was stoned and so, almost, was I. We weren't the only two who were high. There was a man who was visibly drunk. Someone explained that this man had a steady supply of free booze from a contractor who was building a small barrage near the village. I didn't ask what the connection was between the building of the barrage and the supply of free booze. The drunk man asked me to use my 'foreign contacts' to donate money for a bigger temple. There was a murmur all around me as everyone seemed to agree.

'Have your wishes been fulfilled by doing the Trinath Mela?' I asked the assembly.

'Oh, many wishes. So many, you cannot count,' said someone.

'If you believe then he is God; if not, it is a stone,' said the drunk man.

'My prayers have always been heard by Lord Trinath,' said a Mausa. 'Both my sons are now in Kerala, working as truck drivers.'

'After we built the Trinath temple, we got a concrete road...' a man said.

'...and electricity,' another man added.

'Concrete houses from the government. Free!' said a third.

'And running water.'

'But that has stopped now.'

'All politics! Lord Trinath will bring the water back, you'll see.'

'If you sell your vote for Rs 10,000 what will Lord Trinath do?'

'Didn't you listen when the Trinath Book was being read? Lord Trinath can do anything. He can make the blind see and the lame to walk. He can bring a dead man back to life.'

'He is the god of the poor. He's a homely god. You don't need brahmins to do His puja. In our village, we don't have brahmins but still we have Trinath Mela. Anyone can perform his puja.'

Everyone had prasad and went home, their torches flashing in the velvet darkness.

The Bhang Doctors

I think everyone who drinks bhang or smokes ganja claims himself or herself to be a bhang doctor or ganja doctor. They all say that bhang and ganja have medicinal properties and that they've been used as medicine for thousands of years. Ayurveda, they say, confirms this (which is true). I'm not sure if any of them ever read anything related to bhang and ganja at all—whether in some Veda or some medical journal—but this does not prevent them from making pronouncements about the wonder drugs.

I did the same when I was addicted to bhang and ganja. They were cures for almost every ailment, I would say, and they had no side effects. I think I did this to justify my addiction. Many others do it for the same reason.

A lot of the people I know who are regular bhang drinkers also believe that if you drink a bit of bhang before sex you last really long and can give much pleasure to your partner. I can't remember if that's been the case with me. I rarely knew when I'd smoked ganja and when I'd drunk bhang. And I mostly was too far gone in any case.

One woman friend told me recently that she smokes a joint every day to feel relaxed after a day's hard work. I asked if she, too, believed in its medicinal properties, and she replied that she did. 'There are thousands of articles and videos on YouTube about this,' she said.

I'm not sure about thousands, but a search on the internet throws up hundreds of sites selling cannabis-infused oil and tablets for relaxation and sleep. Almost every ayurvedic doctor on the net or the physical world will tell you that the shastras and Puranas contain detailed information about the health benefits and the limitless curative properties of cannabis. But I wonder if it is really so. Because if this were indeed the case, why does Hanuman in the Ramayana fly across oceans and half a continent for the extremely rare Sanjeevani herb—which, again, he could not identify and therefore uprooted an entire mountain?

Or could it be that the Sanjeevani herb was actually a special variety of bhang plant that grew in the Himalayas?

Well, in Odisha at least, it is common belief that bhang is a wonder drug. Many—and not just those who consume it–also consider bhang-ganja to be a gift of the gods. And a gift fit for the gods. Perhaps that is why the government bhang shops in Odisha don't have a notice outside telling people that consumption of bhang is injurious to health, or that it can cause psychological problems. On each bottle of alcohol and every packet of cigarettes, there are written warnings, often with graphic images of disease and death, about the dangers of consuming these products. But you don't find any such warning on the bhang packets they sell.

To my mind, this is both good and sensible.

~

In every town and village of Odisha, you will find a Kabiraj. The dictionary defines Kabiraj as 'an occupational title in the eastern Indian subcontinent'. A dictionary I consulted further explained that 'in the olden days, people traditionally practising Ayurveda were generally called *kabi* or *kobi* in eastern India'.

The Kabirajes of Odisha are great believers in the health benefits of bhang and have a very strong following. They claim to cure everything from cold and cough to cancer and many people go to them for medical advice–among them, a fair number of the high and mighty.

One of the oldest political leaders of the state has gone on the television on several occasions to proclaim that there is nothing wrong in drinking bhang; in fact, it does him a whole lot of good. It helps him clear his bowels, for instance. Take a glass of lassi with some bhang, bel, ripe banana and cottage cheese at night, he says, and the shit comes out smooth and easy in the morning as a long, thick, beautiful turd. Reporters laugh at his funny interviews and people call him Bhang Aja–Bhang Grandfather.

There are many ayurvedic clinics in Odisha that recommend bhang and ganja as medicine. I decided to call a few and visit them, if necessary, to interview them for the book.

The first ayurvedic doctor I called refused to tell me for which treatment he used cannabis. He said I should do my own research, read all the shastras, to find out whether bhang and ganja had medicinal properties or not. He had no doubt that they did, but he wouldn't agree to give me an interview on camera or even on the phone.

Visits to other such establishments yielded varying results: At a clinic in the centre of Bhubaneswar, I was told that cannabis does indeed have medicinal properties, but I should go do a Google search for details.

One clinic had ten or 15 images of various gods outside the entrance. Inside, a lady was doing a puja, ringing a little prayer bell. I waited for her to finish, then asked her if there was a doctor to whom I could speak about ayurvedic medicines. She replied that they no longer gave medicines, they only gave a relaxing ayurvedic massage and I must try one. When I asked if she knew anything about bhang and ganja being used as medicine, she said I should pray to any god of my choice for at least a few minutes every day and that would help me feel relaxed and have a good night's sleep.

Another lady ayurvedic doctor had no hesitation recommending bhang for sound sleep. She took a little bhang herself for the purpose, she said. Just a little, every evening. The shastras said many good things about bhang, I should study them. But bhang was not to be used directly as medicine; it had to be purified to take out all its harmful effects. Bhang was an important ingredient in traditional medicine, she said, and traditional medicine had cured millions of people of all kinds of ailments.

On calling another Ayurvedic clinic, I got an older, gravelly-voiced woman on the phone. Her father had been a vaidya, she told me, and after he died, she had continued his noble work. Her family had been dispensing ayurvedic medicine for over 70 years. I asked her about bhang. 'It has many good qualities,' she said without hesitation. 'Bhang is used to make Nidrodaya Rasa for good sleep and also to purify the blood. We don't use it, but it is used by many good people and many Ayurvedic medicine books mention its usage and contain formulas to make medicines with it.' Could I meet her for more information, I asked, to which she replied, 'There are many books on the subject, you must read them. They are all available in the market or online.'

Another vaidya I called told me that his clinic had a long history. 'It was started in 1872 by my great grandfather's father, we have continued his legacy. Many shastras mention the medicinal properties of bhang and ganja. The herb is purified and the neurotoxins are taken out before it is used in medicines. But you see, a lot of people use it directly and get addicted to it, they use it as a drug, not as medicine. That is wrong.' He promised to send me a list of all the diseases that could be cured by cannabis, and share details about making various medicines. I waited for days, but nothing came from him.

The widespread belief in the curative properties of cannabis notwithstanding, in 2019, the Odisha government rejected proposals from pharmaceutical industries to allow cultivation of cannabis, saying it might cause harm to the people. Ganja cultivation continues to be an illegal activity in the state.

On 10 May 2023, following a petition filed by a religious body, the Odia Language, Literature & Culture Department directed all district collectors and superintendents of police to 'take necessary steps' to prohibit the use of ganja in Shiva temples. 'Restriction will be imposed on the use of Ganja in all the Shaivite temples of the state,' an official statement said.

I wonder if Lord Shiva approved.

~

During my research online, I found many interesting sites that champion the responsible use of cannabis. Hempcann.in tells us:

> Cannabis is an ancient plant and has been used by human beings since the last 2,500 years. In Ayurveda, cannabis is referred to as Vijaya, meaning the Conqueror. It regulates the body's endocannabinoid system (ECS), the immune system and enhances psychological wellbeing. It is the most versatile plant in pharmacology...
>
> [The extract] of the cannabis plant is a great medicine for managing a range of diseases and

symptoms like: Cancer, Nausea & Anorexia, Diabetes, Irregular Bowel Syndrome, Cardiovascular Diseases, Anxiety & Depression, Pain Management, Neurological Disorders, Neurodegenerative Diseases, Glaucoma, PTSD, OCD, Psoriasis & Other Skin Disorders, Asthma, Chronic Kidney Disease, Auto-immune Disorders, Diarrhoea, Migraine, Drug De-addiction, Reproductive Disorders, Stress, Insomnia...

Hemp seeds help in regulating blood pressure and cholesterol... It is great for hair and skin due to the presence of Omega fatty acids. It's anti-oxidant properties rejuvenate our skin.

I don't know how much of this is true, but my research also led me to scholarly articles online which said similar things. I reproduce below excerpts from an article by Shri C. Dwarkanath, Adviser in Indigenous Systems of Medicine, Government of India, Ministry of Health, New Delhi' dated 1 January 1965':

Introduction

Opium and cannabis have been employed as therapeutic agents by the Ayurveda and Unani Tibbi systems of medicine for over ten centuries. There is no direct evidence to show that these drugs were recognized by Ayurveda prior to the eighth century AD However, a reference in *Vartika* and *Ashtadhyayi* of Panini by Katyayana shows that *bhang* (cannabis) was known in India as early as the fourth and third centuries BC. The uses of this drug have not been referred to in any contemporary works on medicine. Sushruta (surgeon, about the fourth century BC) stated that sura (alcohol) should be used before a surgical operation to produce insensibility to pain. Charaka–the internist–prescribed the administration of one or the other of the alcoholic drinks, viz., *sura, sidhu, arishta, madhu, madira* or *asava*–to a full-term pregnant woman, after the extraction of a dead foetus, with a view to making her insensible to pain. There is no reference in the works of these authorities to the use of cannabis or opium as analgesics. This leads to the conclusion that even though bhang (cannabis) was known during the contemporary period, it was not recognized as a therapeutic agent by surgeons and physicians of those times. References to opium are not available in the Vedas, Puranas and early Ayurvedic medical classics such as *Charaka Samhita* (third to second century BC), *Sushruta Samhita* (fifth to fourth century BC), the twin works of Vagbhata (fifth century AD), viz., *Ashtanga Hridaya* and *Ashtanga Samgraha*.

References to both cannabis and opium appear in veterinary and medical works belonging to the 12th to 13th centuries AD onwards. Jayaditya, in his work, *Ashwavaidyaka*–a treatise on the treatment of horses–makes a reference to opium. This work is considered to have been written sometime during the 12th and 13th centuries AD. *Sharangadhara Samhita,* a compendium of therapeutics (13th century AD), has included medicaments titrated with the fresh extract of *bhang.* Authoritative Ayurvedic works on materia medica such as *Dhanwantari nighantu* (8th century AD), *Madanapala nighantu* (1374 AD) and *Raja nighantu* (1450 AD) have described the properties, actions and indications of both cannabis and opium. Bhavamishra (15th century AD), a contemporary of Paracelsus, has in his compendium on medicine and therapeutics, *Bhavaprakasha,* described the properties, actions, indications and formulations of both cannabis and opium. Much later, Ayurvedic medical works have given increasing importance to these two drugs and included them in a large number of formulations.

The foregoing notwithstanding, Indian legends and traditions have associated cannabis and opium with the Shaivite and Shaktiya cults. Sadhus and yogis belonging to these cults have been known to use either cannabis or opium or both to induce concentration of mind towards meditation on the supreme being. Even so, bhang in particular, prepared in different forms, has been utilized in religious rituals by certain sections of people. In some parts of India, bhang prepared in the form of a syrup is consumed on such festive occasions as Holi and Shivratri.

It would appear that cannabis and opium have also been employed by traditional folk medicine in the treatment of diseases even as early as the fourth to third century BC. During the last two centuries, traditional folk medicine and the classical Indian medicine have become almost synonymous. Many drugs, including those containing cannabis and opium, have entered into the practice of classical Ayurveda.

Cannabis and Opium in Unani Tibbi

The Unani Tibbi system would appear to have recognized cannabis and opium as therapeutic agents much earlier than Ayurveda did. The Ayurvedic system appears to have adopted cannabis and opium from Arabian medicine, which was brought to India round about the ninth century AD by the Muslims. Arabian medicine came to be known in India as 'Unani Tibbi' in view of its Greek origin. Dioscorides (first century AD) had described both cannabis and opium, and he is seen to have made use of them for therapeutic purposes. Galien (138-201 AD) and Rhazes (865-925 AD) have given detailed descriptions of these drugs, their actions, therapeutics and uses. Authoritative Arabic and Persian medical works such as *Firdous-ul-Hikmat* and *Mujarbat Qanoon* have not only described the properties of these drugs, but also included a number of formulations containing them.

> It would appear that potions containing cannabis and linctus containing opium were popular in Arabia, Persia and Muslim India. The Unani Tibbi system of medicine in India has a large number of preparations containing these two drugs.

There is a great deal of fascinating information that Dwarakanath provides. I would recommend that you read it; the 15 or 20 minutes would be very well spent. The full article can be found on the website of the United Nations Office on Drugs and Crime (https://www.unodc.org/unodc/en/data-and-analysis/bulletin/bulletin_1965-01-01_1_page004.html)

An Opium Journal

During my frequent visits to the Excise Department office for research on bhang and ganja, I gathered some facts about the use of a related, popular drug—opium. The most interesting information was about opium cards and the government opium de-addiction programme in Odisha.

During my days in Puri's Beach Road area, I had tried opium with black tea and had also smoked it with tobacco. But I had never heard of the opium-user cards. Once I learned of these, I simply had to find out more about the use of this ancient—and at one time almost a household—drug. And this led me to some opium addicts, and to officials in charge of the process of opium procurement and distribution through the Odisha Excise Department.

The Opium Cutter

I am the opium cutter in the Central Bhang and Opium Gola in Cuttack, Odisha. I am around 60 years old. I can tell you my exact age after looking at my Aadhaar card. I started working as the opium cutter around 1984. My father had been working as the opium cutter here since 1955. When he was too old and the time came to retire, he requested the big sahebs in the Excise Department to appoint me as the opium cutter.

My father taught me how to make the big bulky mass of hard opium soft by massaging it with mustard oil and then cutting it into one-gram tablets. He told me that one day, my job could be a permanent government job if I kept at it diligently. I was a young boy and was good at learning the art of making opium tablets quickly.

I have heard about the opium card, which is given to people who need opium for health reasons. I don't know when the opium card was first issued, but my father says it's been there since his days of work as the opium cutter. I also don't know why the opium cards were issued, but I have heard that people suffering from asthma were also issued these opium cards. No new opium cards are being issued now. I think the cards were issued till the year 2005. I am not sure why the Excise Department stopped issuing new cards.

Many people used the cards just to get the opium and use it as a drug. They had no health issues at all. Those days, we used to process around 50 kilograms of opium every year, now many card holders have died, and we only process ten to 12 kilograms a year.

I have never gotten addicted to opium, but when you work with opium the entire day, you really get high on the smell of it. Sometimes, I end up eating biscuits and drinking tea with the same unwashed hands which I used to process the opium. When I am working the mustard oil into the opium, I get very high sometimes. I have never used any face masks or hand gloves to process the opium. During the hot summer days, when you work with mustard oil to process the crude opium, the smell makes it unbearable to work. Maybe the oil enters through the skin and takes some of the opium with it. I even sleep for a day or two after work. I have gotten high without consuming opium, and sometimes, I think how high I would get if I actually did consume it. I have heard that people put opium in their mouth and drink it with tea, but I have never tried it.

I have never heard of anyone dying of an opium overdose, but I have often heard of people dying of adulterated alcohol.

When I started working around 1984-85, I was getting paid Rs 12 to process one kilogram of opium. I was getting very little money every month, even after making thousands of opium tablets. I worked on a daily wage basis and could get work for 20 to 22 days a month at the Bhang Gola. Sometimes, I used to cycle 30 kilometres from my home to the Bhang Gola, only to return home without any work. Those days, I was young, I could cycle easily; now I take the bus.

We were four opium cutters during those days, now I am the only one. I have a helper, too. His father also worked as an opium cutter, but the son hasn't learned the art. I am teaching him slowly, not that anyone has asked me to teach him. He is good. He will learn the art soon.

The salary of an opium cutter is not enough, but what can I do? I manage somehow because I have farm land and other ancestral property and a house left by my father to stay in. In my village, people sometimes ask my children: 'Where does your father work? Excise department? Must be making a lot of black money.' But my salary can't even fill our stomachs. Believe me, I can't even afford to buy new clothes for myself. I get

Rs 351 a day for the eight days that I work to make the opium tablets, now the number of opium card holders is very less, so I only get to work eight days a month.

I have often thought of leaving this job and selling milk or something—anything where I can make better money. But time seems to have flown by even as I was thinking, and now I am too old to do anything other than making opium tablets of one gram each.

I kept working, believing my father's words that one day my job might become a permanent government job with all the government benefits and a handsome salary and a pension after retirement, but that never happened.

My father also worked all his life as an opium cutter and died as a daily wage worker for the Excise Department and the government. Now I am also nearly dead working as a daily wage worker. I got married, had children and they are getting old and I am still waiting for the government to make my job permanent and give me all the benefits.

Many people come asking me for opium; they offer money, but I have always asked people not to take opium and to take medicine instead if they are not feeling well. I know if you take opium, you feel energetic, unlike bhang, which makes you sleepy. I have also seen many women taking opium, sometimes both husband and wife take opium.

I am not sure if there will be an opium cutter after me. I will teach others if the sahibs ask me to teach opium tablet-making to someone, just like my father taught me. My father was picked up from a ganja shop by an excise officer to work as an opium cutter along with a few others when the government started issuing opium cards.

My father never got addicted to opium. I have not heard of anyone from the department getting addicted to opium or opium being stolen from the Bhang Gola ever.

I have written many letters, applications to the sahibs to make me a permanent government employee but I have had no reply. I have filed a case in the High Court of Orissa in Cuttack, requesting the government to regularize my service and give me government benefits. It's been three years, but nothing has happened yet. I have cried a lot in front of the sahibs. Many sahibs have made promises, but nothing has happened. Many others have died waiting for a permanent job. I might also die waiting.

Card-carrying Opium Addicts

The Odisha Opium Deaddiction Programme of the Excise Department has been in place for many decades now, though the Excise Department of Odisha stopped issuing new opium deaddiction cards in 2004 or 2005. But there are still more than 200 'active' opium addicts in the state at the time of writing. Odisha had 236 opium addict card holders alive as of 25 December 2022, with an annual uptake of 22 kilos and 475 grams.

Opium deaddiction cards were issued by the Department of Excise on the recommendation of the Chief Medical Officer (CMO) of each district. It was the CMO's job to certify that a person did not respond to other medicines and to decide the amount of opium to be given after a careful medical examination. Most cards were issued to older addicts but in some cases, they were also issued to younger people with severe pulmonary conditions such as asthma or chronic bronchitis.

The Government Opium and Alkaloid Works situated in the state of Uttar Pradesh is the oldest opium factory in India and supplies medicinal opium to the Odisha Excise Department's Central Bhang and Opium Gola in Cuttack. Earlier, an excise inspector would travel to Ghazipur in Uttar Pradesh with a formal requisition from the Excise Department of Odisha with the exact quantity needed for consumption by the opium card holders under the Odisha Opium Deaddiction Programme. But after the recent Coronavirus pandemic, the amount is sent via insured Speed Post.

Once the opium comes to the Central Bhang and Opium Gola, the opium cutter gets to work, cuts the opium in to small pieces and weighs them. Then the small pieces of opium are placed in-between two square rubber flats and pressed hard to make them thin. Then the thin crust of opium is turned into one-gram round tablets, which are then wrapped and packed into a specially designed square transparent plastic container, produced and printed in the government press of the state government of Odisha. Each transparent plastic container has a unique number to trace it and a unique blue colour to identify it easily. Each container has 25 one-gram black opium tablets.

The opium tablets are processed and packed on

every Monday and Tuesday of a week. Excise inspectors from different districts of the state then come to collect the district quota in person from the Central Bhang and Opium Gola. The district excise office has a fixed date to distribute these opium tablets to the card-holding addicts. The opium card holders come with their cards to the respective excise station to collect their quota. The opium given to each addict according to his or her quota is carefully entered in the opium card and the card holder signs against each entry. Everything is done manually. Since these are subsidised, the opium addicts pay only four rupees for each gram of opium.

The minimum quota of subsidised opium that a card-holding addict receives is five grams, and the maximum can be as high as 25 grams. The opium card is renewed every year. Once an opium addict dies, the opium card is surrendered to the Excise Department.

The Opium Card-holding Goldsmith

My father lived more than 102 years and was addicted to opium, I was not very healthy as a child, I suffered from asthma and other respiratory problems. My father started giving me a bit of opium as medicine when I was 12.

Father said he had started taking opium at the age of 15. He had a deaddiction card. After he died, I applied for my own opium deaddiction card around the year 1999. Since then, I have been getting 15 grams of opium every month from the Excise Department. Now I am getting old, and I need a few more grams of opium every month. I would be very happy if the department would increase my quota to 20 grams a month. My father's quota was 25 grams per month.

I take two doses of half a gram of opium every day: once in the morning and once in the evening. I suffer from asthma, so my doctors also suggested I continue taking opium. I like my opium with tea, not with coffee.

I have no other diseases because I take opium

regularly. Opium is a very good medicine. Many people suffering from diarrhoea and even chronic pain from cancer come to me and ask me to give them a bit from my quota of opium. Sometimes, I do give them some because I can't bear to see people in pain. But how many can I help? When I don't get my full quota of opium, I can't move at all, I can't work.

Once, an excise officer forgot to give me my quota and went away on leave to his native village, I was without my opium for three days. I got sick and I had to be put on a bed next to the toilet because I had to keep going to the toilet. My brothers and other family members took me to meet the collector, and the collector summoned the excise officer and told him to take the next available bus to his office and give me my quota of opium. So, I survived, or else I could have died that time. From that day onwards, the department makes sure that I get my quota on time, whatever happens.

I can walk ten kilometres after taking my opium, I can stay without food for a few days and keep working as well. I can see very clearly because when you eat opium, your eyesight improves—my father could see very clearly at the age of 100, he was a goldsmith just like me and could work without any aid on very detailed gold ornament designs. No matter what comes in life, if you are on opium, you are always calm and can face all the difficult situations.

I am married, I have two healthy children. My father was married twice and had 18 children, two from the first wife and after her death, 16 from my mother, all healthy. Opium makes a man strong.

My wife also wants to make an opium card for herself, but the department doesn't approve of it. They say that they have stopped giving these cards now. Can you help, sir? Her health will improve.

We had more than 100 opium card holders in the town but now only two are alive. All opium addicts lived around 85 to 95 years. Opium doesn't kill anybody; it is a very good medicine. I had this other opium addict friend who was around 75 years old. One night, while he was sleeping, the ceiling fan fell on his head and he died. It's the fan that killed my friend, not the opium...People say, if a snake bites me, the snake will die but not me.

My father sometimes gave opium to all my sisters and brothers when they were ill as children, but no one got addicted except me. I was very close to my father. He gave me a bit of opium every now and then so that I wouldn't get tired.

Another friend who was also an opium addict lived more than 100 years like my father; his was a natural death from old age. I wish the big officers in the Excise Department would just listen to people like me and increase their quota of opium; it will help older people like me.

The Woman Who Survived Cholera by Eating Opium

My name is Parvati. I don't remember exactly when I became addicted to opium. I was around 30 or 31 years old when I fell very ill with cholera. My father admitted me into the district cholera hospital for treatment. The doctors kept me on a drip: 70 or 80 saline bottles, one after the other, for days, but my diarrhoea just wouldn't stop. I was in the hospital for three months, and everybody said I was not going to survive. I was in a very serious condition, sir; the doctors had no hope left. My father was an opium addict with a government opium addict card, and when everything else failed, he asked me to lick a bit of his opium, and miraculously, my health improved.

I kept taking a little opium after that, and by the time I had recovered from cholera, I think I had become addicted to opium. I don't hide anything; I always tell the truth. Don't feel bad about the way I talk, sir; I am an open person. I like opium.

Every day, I eat half a gram of opium twice. Since the government only gives me ten grams of opium every month, I fall short by five grams, which I am then forced to buy from outside. But the opium I get from the open market is not even close to the quality opium I get from the government.

My father gave me opium to me to cure my cholera, but I got addicted, and now I can't give it up, sir. It would be better if I were given a little more of it. I say everything openly, sir, don't feel bad. A little more opium would be good for me. I don't have any other health problems, but when I don't have opium, I just keep sneezing and get teary-eyed. Once I eat my opium, I am fresh again.

But I feel ashamed when people say: 'Look! A woman is eating opium.' Now, many women drink and smoke, but I am from a different time. My father lived for more than 80 years eating opium. One day, he had a heart attack while making paan, and he died.

I don't take any other drugs, sir. I can't stop taking opium now. I give thanks to that superintendent, Pani Babu, who made my opium card, I still remember him.

An Opium Card (Or, Permit 'for Eating Opium' on Medical Grounds)

FORM O.P. III
(See rule 20(2))

Sadgar. 'A' Class

Permit No. 1|2003

ermit for the possession of opium for personal consumption in the State of Orissa

A) 1) Permit-holder's name:- Sri [redacted]

2) Father's/Husband name:- Late [redacted]

3) Religion or caste:- Hindu

4) Apparent age :- 65 years

5) Address in full:- Vill- [redacted] [redacted], Cuttack

6) Occupation :- Cultivation

) Purpose for which the permit is granted:- For eating Opium

) Reference to medical certificate:-

1) Name and address of the Medical Board which granted the certificate:- C.D.M.O, Cuttack

2) Date of Certificate:- Vide letter no. 4340 dt 29.4.20

3) Drug recommended:- Medicinal opium

4) Quantity recommended per month:- 15 Tolas per month

5) Personal identification marks of the permit holder as verified by the medical Board:-
1)
2)
3)

This permit is granted under and subject to the rovisions of Narcotic Drugs and Psychotropic Substances Act, 1985 and the rules, regulations and orders ade thereunder to Sri [redacted] Banava, Cuttack hereinafter referred to as "the permit-holder" on ayment of a fee of Rs. 10/- Vide challan 25 dt 9-7-03 authorising him to uy, posses, transport and consume opium subject to the llowing conditions:-

CONDITIONS

This permit shall remain in force from 1.11.03 to 30.10.2004 (both days inclusive).

. The permit-holder shall as soon as possible present his permit before the local Inspector or Sub-inspector of Excise for his countersignature and in any case ot later than one month from the receipt of this ermit.

3) 1) The permit-holder shall not purchase during any one month opium exceeding 7 (Seven) grams;

Provided that this quantity may be reduced during the currency of the permit in accordance with the provision in Orissa Narcotic Drugs and Psychotropic Substances Rule, 1989.

2) The permit-holder shall not possess at any one time more than 5 grams of opium.

4) 1) The permit-holder shall not obtain his supplies of opium from any place except from a depot established under rule 24 of Orissa Narcotic Drugs and Psychotropic Substances Rules, 1989.

2) The permit-holder shall get the details of the purchase entered on the reverse of the permit by the Officer-in-charge of the depot, before he removes from the depot the opium purchased by him.

3) No opium other than opium obtained under this permit shall be transported, possessed or consumed by the permit-holder.

5) The opium purchased under this permit shall neither be used by any person other than the permit-holder nor shall it be used for any purpose other than the purpose for which this permit is granted.

6) The privileges of purchase, transport and possession of opium granted under this permit shall extend only so far as they are incidental to its consumption in accordance with this permit.

7) The permit shall be non-transferable and may be suspended or cancelled in accordance with the provisions of Orissa Narcotic Drugs and Psychotropic Substances Rules, 1989.

8) In case the permit is cancelled during its currency or is not renewed on its expiry, the whole of the unconsumed stock of opium shall forthwith be surrendered to the Collector or authorised officer.

Granted this 23rd day of Oct. 2003

Seal

Signature or left hand thumb impression of the permit holder.

[illegible] 28/10/2003 ... authorised Officer

Countersigned.

Inspector/Sub-Inspector of [illegible]

(Reverse of the permit)

The Abolition of Opium Smoking in India

(Fragments from a 1955 article by Sir Ram Nath Chopra and I.C. Chopra on the banning and the 'quasi-medical use' of opium in India)*

In India, two preparations of opium have generally been used for smoking; madak and chandu. The use of madak has been considered to be much more extensive than that of chandu, and in most parts of the country, this preparation was smoked. The following is, briefly, the method employed for its preparation: Raw opium is mixed with water, which is then heated to boiling point. The boiling is continued, and the impurities which form as a scum on the surface of the boiling fluid are gradually removed. The heating is continued till a thick suspension is formed. This is then strained through a piece of cloth, and charred leaves of Acacia arabica (babul) are

---

*Source: https://www.unodc.org/unodc/en/data-and-analysis/bulletin/bulletin_1957-01-01_3_page002.html

gradually mixed with it till it assumes the consistency of a thick, stiff paste. This mass is then rolled into small balls called madak golis, which are available for smoking purposes. As a rule, two and a half ounces of madak are prepared from one ounce of opium. Sometimes, instead of babul leaves, leaves of Phyllanthus emblica (amla), Acacia leucophloea Wild (safed babul) and Piper betle Linn. (paan) are used. In the former days, burnt gold or silver threads (kalabatoo) were sometimes added to the mass, as it was supposed that these imparted to the mixture aphrodisiac and tonic properties.

Chandu, chandul, or clarified opium, is a stronger preparation and was only used in India by persons who were heavy smokers. Chandu is prepared by boiling a strained solution of opium in water until it becomes thick in consistency. As the concentration proceeds, crusts form on the surface of the simmering mass. These are removed as they form until, finally, a thick mass of the consistency and appearance of coal tar is obtained. This is the "smokable extract" and is the chandu or chandul of opium smokers. The chandu commonly smoked is often adulterated by the addition of dross scraped from chandu pipes, which has a high morphine content.

A third preparation—rarely used—was opium dross, which is the residue left in the pipe when chandu or madak is smoked.

Unlike opium eaters, who generally seek solitude in order to indulge in their habit, opium smokers prefer to smoke in the company of other addicts. Furthermore, the requisite paraphernalia is often beyond the reach of the average smoker; an additional difficulty is the absence of a suitable place where addicts can retire for a smoke. As a result, smoking dens providing all facilities have existed probably ever since the habit of smoking originated.

[...]

From the very early days of the establishment of British authority in India, the government of India gradually extended its control over the production, transport and sale of opium. In 1813, there was passed the first Bengal regulation regarding consumption in India, the government enunciating its policy of restricting the habit of opium eating by obtaining the maximum revenue from the minimum consumption and declaring that it was desirous of countenancing only to the narrowest extent possible a habit which it found itself unable to eradicate. The attitude of the government of India towards the general question of opium consumption, which persisted till 1947, was well expressed by the following passage in a despatch addressed to the Secretary of State by Lord Hardinge's government in 1911: "The prohibition of opium eating in India we regard as impossible, and any attempt at it is fraught with the most serious consequences to the people and the Government. We take our stand unhesitatingly on the conclusion of the Royal Commission which reported in 1895, viz., that the opium habit as a vice scarcely exists in India, that opium is extensively used for medical and quasi-medical purposes, in some cases with benefit, and for the most part without injurious consequences; that the non-medical uses are so interwoven with the medical uses that it would not be practicable to draw a distinction between them in the distribution and sale of the drug; and that it is not necessary that the growth of the poppy and the manufacture and sale of opium in British India should be prohibited except for medical purposes. Whatever may be the case in other countries, centuries of inherited experience have taught the people of India discretion in the use of the drug, and its misuse is a negligible feature in Indian life. Even if it were possible to suppress the cultivation of opium in India, geographical and political limitations would place it beyond our power to prevent illicit import and consumption on a serious scale."

Since the government recognized that opium consumption in India could not be entirely suppressed, it pursued a declared policy of restricting the habit within the narrowest possible limits.

[...]

Since 1891, opium smoking on licensed premises was prohibited, and the sale of prepared opium was absolutely prohibited throughout the whole of British India. By provincial rules made under the Opium Act of 1878, the manufacture of smoking preparations was forbidden except by an individual for his own use from opium lawfully in his possession and only to the extent of one tola (3/8 oz) at a time. Under Indian conditions, a tola represents little more than one or two days' average dose for a smoker of low-grade chandu and is a good deal short of the daily dose required by a habitual and confirmed smoker. In consultation with the provincial governments, it was also decided that this maximum limit of private possession of opium smoking preparations should be reduced to a quantity to be determined for each province by its own government with regard to local circumstances. Since 1911, the issue price at which opium was being sold to the consumer was raised to a considerable extent in every province, and the maximum limit of private possession of both raw and prepared opium was reduced.

By 1920-21, the limit of private possession of opium smoking preparations in the case of individuals was reduced in the British provinces to one tola (in the case of Bombay, it was one tola). Similarly, the maximum amount of opium for smoking allowed to an assembly of persons was reduced. It may be pointed out that as of 1911, such an assemblage was not illegal so long as the total quantity of opium used did not exceed the aggregate of one tola apiece, which each of the participants was entitled to possess, subject in some provinces to a maximum of five tolas, even though the collective number of smokers was more than five. By 1920-21, the maximum amount of opium for smoking allowed to an assembly of persons, however large, was one tola in the majority of the British provinces (in Bombay, it was 1/2 tola; in Bengal, it was two tolas; in Bihar and Orissa, it was 2 1/2 tolas).

[...]

The official position by 1945 as regards opium smoking in both British India and the Indian states had advanced considerably towards total prohibition...

[...]

[The] constitution of the Republic...was promulgated in January 1950. Article 47 of the Constitution lays down as a directive principle of state policy that the state government and Parliament of India, and the government and legislature of each of the states and of local or other authorities within the territory of India or under the control of the government of India shall endeavour to bring about prohibition of the consumption—except for medical purposes—of intoxicating drinks and of drugs which are injurious to health.

Under Paragraph 3 of Article 19 of the Opium Protocol of 1953, the Government of India has made a declaration to the effect that the smoking of opium will not be permitted except, for their lifetime, by addicts not under 21 years of age, registered by the appropriate authorities for that purpose on or before 30 September 1953. In pursuance of this declaration, the government of India issued instructions to all the state governments, requesting them to take immediate steps, both legislative and administrative, whichever might be necessary, to announce that the registration of opium smokers, for whatever reasons, would be stopped completely after 30 September 1953, and that only those who registered themselves on medical grounds by 30 September 1953 would be permitted to smoke so long as they survive, subject to their fulfilling certain conditions.

The position reached by each state by 31 December 1949 is summarized below:

[The article by Ram Nath and IC Chopra then gives a list of all the states of the Indian Union as of 1949 and the laws in these states relating to opium consumption. I have excerpted the details of a few, including Odisha, below.]

Assam: The smoking of opium and possession of

prepared opium are totally prohibited under The Assam Opium Smoking Act, 1927.

Andhra: No addict registered himself as a smoker by 30 December 1953.

Bihar: The Bihar and Orissa Opium Smoking Act (II of 1928) has been in force for over 20 years. As the first step, smoking opium and the manufacture or possession of prepared opium were prohibited, except by persons who applied for, and were granted, registration as addicts. No fresh registration of addicts has been permitted since 31 December 1931...

Bombay: The first step to control opium smoking was taken in 1936 with the enactment of the Bombay Opium Smoking Act (XX of 1936), which, by prohibiting smoking of opium in assembly, enabled opium smoking dens to be suppressed. The final action to give effect to the policy of total abolition was taken under the Bombay Prohibition Act, 1949. Possession of opium (except opium to be legally used for medical or scientific purposes) by any person other than a permit holder is prohibited. Permits to possess opium in any form for personal consumption are issued only to persons certified by a medical board constituted by the government, as requiring opium for some specific medical reason...

Orissa: In the territories formerly included in the Province of Bihar and Orissa, control over opium smoking has been in force since 1928 under the Bihar and Orissa Opium Smoking Act (II of 1928.) In 1947, this Act was replaced by The Orissa Opium Smoking Act (XVI of 1947). The smoking of opium and the possession of prepared opium are totally prohibited.

[...]

For weaning the opium addicts from their habit, the All-India Narcotics Conference, which was held in 1956, made the following recommendation:

- The medical permits will be issued only by an appointed medical authority with a view to (a) progressively weaning the addicts, and for (b) relieving pain in case of disease.
- The medical permit must not prescribe a quota of more than five tolas a month. This quantity should be automatically reduced by eighths every quarter, subject to the minimum of 1/8 tola every three months.

Into the Ganja Fields

Excise Officers Share Their Knowledge

Legend has it that sometime in 1990, a man from Punjab came in a helicopter and landed deep inside the Maoist-dominated forests of Redhakhol in Odisha and struck a deal with the Maoists to start marijuana farming on a large scale.

How successful had he been? How much ganja was grown in these areas? Who grew it?

Filing a Right to Information (RTI) application would have been difficult, so I decided to go to the Excise Commissioner's Office in Bhubaneswar and try to find someone who could help me get some information. Perhaps help me travel to the area, too.

The afternoon I first arrived at the Excise Commissioner's office in Bhubaneswar, the counting for an important by-election was in progress, and there was much excitement–the ruling party's pride was at stake. The Excise Commissioner wasn't available, but it was surprisingly easy to meet the Deputy Commissioner of Excise. He guided me to another office in charge of all the matters related to ganja/bhang and opium. He said they would be 'the right people' for me to meet.

The officer there met me and politely said he had all the information I needed, but permission to let me access it would have to come from the Excise Commissioner himself. In the course of the conversation, he told me that he was also from Puri and talked about how Puri has a long history of bhang consumption—eating sweets or cottage cheese with bhang is an almost universal ritual in Puri.

Around 5.30 pm, news of the ruling-party candidate's victory in the by-poll came in, and I was told that I should stay the night because the 'Burra Sahib', the Commissioner, would definitely come to the office the next morning.

I reached the Excise Commissioner's office at ten the next morning. The office assistant asked me to wait.

The Burra Sahib came in around 10.15. I asked the office assistant, 'Can I go in now?'

'Not now,' he said, shocked. 'Only after he takes his morning tea.'

Finally, the office assistant was asked to send me in.

'What do you want?' Excise Commissioner asked when I went in.

'I want to know some more about the government bhang shops and other excise matters for a book I am writing,' I replied.

'Sure, we can help, but we are not giving more bhang shop licenses. We are only renewing the old ones,' he said. 'Our society is full of hypocrites. Punishing young people for consuming drugs won't stop drug abuse. We need to sensitize people on this matter.'

The Commissioner gave me his number and introduced me to his colleague, who he said was the most knowledgeable person on matters pertaining to bhang, ganja and opium. Then he wished me luck and I left his office, and walked with the Knowledgeable Officer to his desk, where another man was already waiting for him.

'So, what do you want to do with all the information?' the Knowledgeable Officer asked.

'I want to write a book on bhang, ganja and opium, sir.'

'It would be my privilege to share my knowledge of excise matters with another knowledgeable person like you, I will try to give you all possible help,' he said. 'Do you want some tea?'

He sent someone to get tea for both of us and for the man who was waiting to talk to him.

'Please give me some time to finish my work of preparing for a meeting and then we can talk,' said the Knowledgeable Officer and got into a conversation with the other man.

As I sipped my tea, I could not help but overhear the other man's problem, which he had brought to the Knowledgeable Officer. Apparently, 75 quintals–that's 7,500 kilograms–of illegal bhang had been seized, but there was no place to store it. The seized bhang was still in the container in which it had been found outside some other officer's quarters, he said, and he feared that it would be eaten by rats or that they might make a nest in it.

Rats high on bhang! I tried not to laugh.

The Knowledgeable Officer was unfazed. Looking at him, I had no doubt he would deal efficiently with the bizarre problem. Meanwhile, he turned to me and mentioned a book related to narcotics and asked if I had read it.

'No sir,' I said. 'I would be obliged if you would lend it to me.'

'Sure,' he said, even as he suggested to the junior office that he should find another, safer storage unit for the seized bhang. It was a simple matter.

Then he turned his attention to me again and handed me a bunch of papers and some books to read.

He also asked me to visit the Excise Commissioner's Office in Cuttack. It was the oldest excise office and also the Central Bhang Gola, he said. All matters related to bhang and opium were handled there.

The next day, I went to the Excise Commissioner's Office–which was also the Central Bhang Gola–in Cuttack. The Officer-in-Charge of the Bhang Gola was out on an excise raid, so I was directed to another senior excise officer's office.

The senior excise officer offered me coffee and wanted to know more about my project.

'So, what are you writing, and how is it going to help the public?'

'I don't know whether it will help the public, sir,' I replied. 'I just want to document interesting information about the Central Bhang Gola and the opium deaddiction programme before it becomes history.'

The officer was happy to be of help. At one point, he said that I should know that although bhang lassi was sold openly everywhere, this was, in fact, completely illegal. 'Anyone can buy up to 120 grams of bhang for personal use but cannot resell it or make any other byproduct from the bhang for sale.'

He also informed me that bhang or ganja that is seized is valued at Rs 10 per gram and opium at

Rs 50 per gram. He offered me a list with the values of all the other related items seized by excise–including empty bottles, cork, poppy, etc.

Our conversation was interrupted when two junior officers came in. The senior excise officer said to them, 'Go file more cases. If you file more cases, I will send you all to Inox to watch a film.'

We all laughed.

I went back to the Central Bhang Gola the following morning, took some pictures, gathered the necessary information I needed carefully and prepared to go back home to Bhubaneswar.

But before leaving Cuttack, I wanted to see the oldest bhang shop that was still operational. I'd been told it was in the Mangalabag area. It was evening when I found the little shop–on the ground floor of a multistoried building in an alley leading to a busy hotel. An old man sat inside with a tray filled with hundreds of globules of bhang paste. Men came in a hurry, paid Rs 10 to Rs 20, swallowed a globule or two with a glass of water and were gone in seconds.

'Do you have any ganja?' I asked the old shop owner.

'No, we only sell bhang,' he replied.

A man sitting next to him said, 'Getting good ganja has become difficult in the city, but you can still find it in some places. No one is going to give it to you, though. Your face is new in this area.'

'How old is this place?' I asked.

'More than a hundred years,' said a customer, pausing mid-flight. 'I'm fifty-fifty-five years old, and I've heard this bhang shop has been here since before my father's birth. Of course, it was not in a modern building like this; it was a small hut in those days.'

'How many people come to take bhang here?'

'Hundreds,' he said, and popped his ball of bhang, drank his water and left.

~

There were many interesting facts and figures I gathered in Cuttack. Particularly revealing was a report on ganja plant destruction in Odisha.

Planting of ganja, or hemp, begins in August-September every year, and the harvest is ready in about six months, around January-February. The Excise Department destroys thousands of acres of illegal ganja plantations every year.

The destruction report for 2021-22 revealed that of the approximately 20,000 acres of ganja plantation destroyed during that financial year, almost half came from four southern districts–Malkangiri, Koraput,

Rayagada and Gajapati, all dominated by Maoists and sharing borders with Andhra Pradesh, Telangana and Chhattisgarh–and the rest from two districts–Kandhamal and Boudh.

I decided to travel to all six districts and see what was happening with my own eyes. I would start with the four southern districts dominated by Maoists.

Seize and Destroy: Three Intoxicants, Three Tables

Seizure of Bhang	
2020–2021	3173.64 kg
2021–2022	3943.49 kg
Seizure of Ganja	
2020–2021	3699.59 kg
2021–2022	18264.13 kg
Seizure of Opium	
2020–2021	24.142 kg
2021–2022	7.6 kg

Hemp Plant Destruction

YEAR WISE HEMP PLANT DESTRUCTION (IN ACREs)

Sl no	District	2019-20	2020-21	2021-22
01	Angul	1.16	5.15	6.65
02	Berhampur	5	70	15
03	Boudh	993	1007	1003.7
04	Deogarh	2		
05	Gajapati	1690.957	4465.542	4381.67
06	Ganjam	43	112	187
07	Kandhamal	7946	9293	9310
08	Koraput	568	666	776.09
09	Malkangiri	3633	5429	2528
10	Rayagada	1103	1169	1566
11	Sambalpur		0.4	0.42
12	Kalahandi			0.1
	Total	**15985**	**22217**	**19774.63**

YEAR WISE HEMP PLANT DESTRUCTION (IN Numbers)

Sl no	District	2019-20	2020-21	2021-22
01	Angul	6862	15260	6897
02	Berhampur	10201	165000	45000
03	Boudh	30303000	3021000	1741638
04	Deogarh	5230		
05	Gajapati	3904122	8931084	8759774
06	Ganjam	62018	112000	280500
07	Kandhamal	4976000	9293000	9310000
08	Koraput	689000	799190	932170
09	Malkangiri	6712600	8837900	10267000
10	Rayagada	177900	1329000	1566000
11	Sambalpur		230	4800
12	Kalahandi			253
	Total	**49816933**	**32503664**	**32914032**

A Raid in Malkangiri

Until the second decade of the 21st century, most parts of the Malkangiri district were cut off from the district headquarters, mainly because the Maoists controlled a majority of the interior villages and didn't allow road construction to happen. Recently, with almost no leadership left, Maoist dominance of the district has weakened. This has resulted in steady development work and road and bridge connectivity, but it has come at a cost—the overwhelming presence of the central and other paramilitary forces can be felt wherever you go.

I decided to fly to the nearest airport in Jeypore, the biggest town in the district of Koraput, which is 512 kilometres from Bhubaneswar and 110 kilometres from the district headquarters of Malkangiri. The airport was very new and had been made operational in just a few months. There was only has one daily flight—a Cessna Grand Caravan EX; a nine-seater—from Bhubaneswar, and one from Visakhapatnam. The airlines asked everyone to pee before boarding the flight as there were no lavatories on the plane. When the pilot was briefing us about the route, weather, and altitude, he also mentioned that we would be flying over the Eastern Ghats and Koraput.

The flight took off around 10 am. I took a nap and opened my eyes to the beautiful Eastern Ghats through the aircraft window. Around ten minutes past 12 pm, the captain announced that we were flying over Koraput and would soon land in Jeypore. Koraput, I knew, is one of the biggest illegal ganja-farming districts of Odisha. Looking through the Cessna's small window, I saw a few patches of scattered fire and smoke rising into the air from the hills below. I wondered if it was the Excise Department burning ganja plantations or some Adivasi villagers clearing forest land for farming.

I landed at the small airport in Jeypore at about half past noon. My friend Guru was waiting to take me to Malkangiri town in his car. He had already arranged for me to go to the villages deep in the forest to see a ganja plantation, but he warned me, 'No one is going to speak to you about ganja farming.'

I had also requested a friend in the government to speak to the excise team and request them to take me along on one of their ganja destruction expeditions.

I had ditched my initial idea of going into the forest with just my friend and some local villagers as my friends in the government said it could get very risky. I spoke to the Excise Department in Malkangiri over the phone, and they assured me of their support and told me that they had also arranged a room in the circuit house for me.

After pit stops for lunch and coffee, we reached the Malkangiri Circuit House, 106 km away, at around 4:30 pm. Guru said that a few years ago, the roads would have been impassable; the Maoists would blow them up using land mines or felled massive trees and used them as roadblocks. But things had improved in the last few years.

In the evening, the Excise Department officer and I had tea together at a tea stall near the circuit house. Another member of the Excise Department joined us and we discussed the next day's expedition to destroy ganja plantations. The officer said we must start before seven in the morning since we had to cover around 95 kilometres by road and then walk another ten kilometres to reach the illegal plantations in the hills in the Chitrakonda block bordering Andhra Pradesh. I was told that the villagers there use government land to cultivate ganja, so that no one can be arrested and charge-sheeted for illegal farming since the land belongs to the Forest Department of Odisha, and it is this department's duty to protect these lands. The forest department, however, denies the existence of any illegal ganja plantations on its land, mainly because it lacks the manpower to keep an eye on the entire forest and cannot admit to failure or dereliction of duty. There's another complication: the Odisha-Andhra Pradesh border is less than ten kilometres away and some parts of the forest are disputed, claimed by both states.

Late evening, the excise officer sent someone to my room with a vegetable curry, a few chapatis, and a bottle of beer. I ate and drank and wrote down the day's experience and went to bed.

I was up around 5.30 in the morning and took a walk and had black tea with black pepper and lemon served by a woman tea-seller. Guru joined me an hour later and took me to a beautiful dosa place, where we only paid Rs 60 for all the dosa and idli we ate. And the food was far superior to what we would have got for twice that amount in a big city.

At around seven, a rattletrap rolled up. The excise officer explained, 'No one would offer a good vehicle to go into the forest for ganja destruction, sir. They fear that they might be attacked or kidnapped or their vehicle burnt to ashes. Even this one was difficult to get. I hope you won't mind too much.'

We stopped at a market to buy water bottles, bananas and some oranges. The officer told me that we wouldn't find anything in the villages inside the forest, and even if the villagers had water and food, they would not give us any or even sell anything to us for good money. 'Why would they, sir?' he asked philosophically. 'We are going to destroy their crops.'

The ganja-plantation-demolition party left Malkangiri town around 7:30 am in three old vehicles, two from the Excise Department and the hired apology of a vehicle. The cargo comprised some 20 people from the Excise Department, ten personnel from the local police station, six daily wage labourers, four bush-cutting machines and around 15 machetes. In a separate truck, for our protection, were 25 jawans from the District Voluntary Force, or DVF. (The DVF, set up in 2009, is a special constabulary unit of Odisha Police, primarily used in anti-Maoist operations.)

All the vehicles travelled around 90 kilometres by road and halted a few kilometres before we reached a small village surrounded by hills and forests. A few DVF jawans stayed back to protect the vehicles, which were sometimes torched or damaged by the villagers as a protest. In recent years, the villagers have violently protested ganja destruction by the Excise Department by throwing stones at the personnel engaged in hacking plants. There is also the fear of ambush or abduction by the Maoists.

After walking for a few kilometres and crossing millet fields, we reached the hills, and the first ganja plantation came into view. When we climbed a slight rise, we saw ganja plantations across the valley, almost as far as the eye could see.

There was also a patch of bare land, about an acre. This had been a forest not a long time ago and had been entirely cleared. The land had then been flattened using an excavator.

One of the excise officers said: 'To clear a patch this size by clearing the forest and to plant ganja would require an investment of more than four or five lakhs. And think about this–our budget for the entire district of Malkangiri is around five lakh rupees. With that, we are supposed to destroy thousands of acres of illegal ganja plantations in this difficult terrain. It's a race against time and a battle already lost, but we keep fighting hard. By the time we get to about half of the illegal plantations, the mafia behind this has easily harvested thousands of quintals of ganja.'

The ganja plants we saw had obviously been tended well. They were planted in straight rows, irrigated well with rubber water pipes travelling miles from the streams in the hills to the valley below, irrigating not only the ganja but also the millet and other crops in the fields of the Adivasis living in the villages. Plenty of fertilizer and pesticides are used to help the ganja plants grow fast and healthy. Organic isn't big in the ganja world. The odd new-age hippie might insist on organically farmed weed, but even this rare specimen of humanity would compromise if supplies dipped or the price rose.

As soon as the ganja-cutting party started hacking the Ganja late that morning, a group of women rushed up out of the village and started shouting. Some wept and cursed the ganja-cutting team in their local dialects, Desia and Koya.

'Why are you killing my crops?' one woman demanded angrily. 'Are you going to pay for my children's food and education?'

Another wailed: 'If you want to hack my plants, then hack my baby with it. How can we survive the year without money?'

A third argued: 'We are not making liquor to kill people; this is just a natural plant. We have been growing it for so long, no one ever came to destroy it. Why are you doing this?'

Someone from the cutting party said to the women: 'Why don't you grow tomato, cauliflower and other vegetables, Mother?'

'Those rot in a few days,' one of the women shot back. 'People don't even pay a rupee for them. We have been growing ganja for years, and it harmed no one. No one bothered us. We were better off without this road to our village. Now you come in your motors and destroy everything.' Then she broke down, overcome with helpless rage and cursed the cutting party. 'May your wives be widowed! May your children fall dead just like my ganja plants cut down by your machines.'

An Adivasi man came forward and said, 'Sir, can't you just destroy half and leave the other half? We have taken big loans from the moneylender in the nearby town, how will we repay them?'

Through the commotion and protests, the cutting team moved carefully up and down the hills. The smell of ganja began to fill the air. As the cutting and hacking progresses, the air becomes thick and heavy with the smell, making you a little high.

Someone said, 'Be careful. Don't uproot the tomato, corn and chilli plants we have planted in between the ganja. This is our food; we are dependent on it until the next season.'

One of the team members picks up a plant and shows it to me. 'See, the flowers have bloomed. That means it is ready for harvesting. If you squeeze these flowers between your palms and they get sticky, that means it's almost ready for harvesting.'

Ganja destruction is slow work, even with a bush-cutting machine. But most of the work is done by men on foot with a machete, keeping in mind the vegetables grown in between the ganja plants. After the cutting, the plants must be incinerated using brushwood–which has to be gathered–and petrol. Leaving the plants lying around would mean the Excise Department making the smugglers' job a lot easier.

By afternoon, arms were tired, backs were aching, the sun was hot, all the fruit had been eaten, and the water bottles were almost empty. The mood had grown worse, the women coming closer and getting angrier and angrier, their voices rising in a potent mixture of grief and rage.

'Shit-eater, piss-drinker,' they screamed. 'May you die vomiting blood. May your children starve as you are making our children starve. May all your wives be widowed.'

One of the women picked on me. She walked beside me, abusing me, saying, 'I could tear you apart with one hand.'

I kept on walking, I walked faster to get away, but she would not give up. She kept pace, challenging me. 'Are you even a man?'

I stopped to say something when a jawan stopped me. 'Don't engage with them. If you say anything, this could escalate into a bloody conflict.'

I held my peace.

Eventually, the ganja-cutting party began to retreat to the vehicles, hoping not to be attacked.

On the way back, I saw many more acres of ganja plants, all ready to be harvested soon. Some plants had been harvested and kept under the sun in an open land to dry, but we ignored them as more and more villagers were gathering, and the ganja-cutting team feared things might get violent.

I saw a man with a shoulder-pole laden on both sides with freshly harvested millet. I stopped him and asked if I could carry the load for a moment. The man smiled, stopped, transferred the shoulder-pole onto my shoulder. I could manage less than 20 steps. It felt like 40 kilograms, I hadn't the strength for it.

A DVF jawan who was watching this said, 'These are hard-working men, sir. This is how they carry ganja on their shoulders and walk hundreds of kilometres over narrow jungle roads to transport ganja to Chhattisgarh, Telangana and Andhra Pradesh, where some other vehicle is ready to transport it to some big city.'

The jawan told me how a home guard was killed by the drug mafia deep inside the forest; how two Adivasis carrying ganja on shoulder-poles were mistaken as Maoists and gunned down.

I asked the young Adivasis whose shoulder-pole I

had tried to carry if he knew anything about the people who invest money in the farming of ganja.

He shrugged and stopped talking.

The excise officials had warned me about this: the villagers never disclose any information about the people who fund these huge farms. There are vague references to local agents in the district who give money to the villagers. If the farm is destroyed by the Excise Department, the farmer can adjust the money he owes the agent against produce from the next farming season.

Other farmers don't grow ganja: they just take care of the plants and get paid per plant.

During the season, one kilogram of ganja fetches Rs 3,000 to Rs 5,000; by the time it gets to a city like Mumbai or Bangalore, it can be around Rs 50,000 to Rs 1,00,000 per kilogram in the open market.

An excise officer told me a story about a guy who had come to Malkangiri on a motorbike from Delhi through the border town of Jagdalpur in Chhattisgarh. He was caught taking back a little under 20 kilograms of ganja in a backpack on his way back to Delhi. The motorbike was registered in someone else's name, and since the ganja was less than 20 kilograms, which is not considered a high commercial quantity, the guy got bail within a month or two.

'Malkangiri has turned into a shopping mall for ganja buyers from around the country,' the excise officer said.

It was almost three in the afternoon by the time we reached Chitrakonda. The officer showed me the Balimela Reservoir built on the river Sileru and said, 'Sir, this was built jointly by the Odisha and Andhra Pradesh governments with Russian assistance.'

I was very hungry by this time. Lunch was rice, dal and cabbage curry with fish from the reservoir at a small canteen for forest officials. My hands smelt of ganja even after I had washed them with soap and water for quite some time. I was surprised how much I minded the strong smell of ganja in my food.

On reaching the Malkangiri Circuit House, the excise officer informed me that the Excise Department of Koraput was going on a ganja-cutting drive the next day. 'I have already spoken to my counterpart in Koraput. I told him you wanted to go out as part of the team, and they have agreed.'

I decided to take the next bus to Koraput. Guru came on his motorbike, and we reached the bus stop around 6 pm. The bus stop was rich with the smell of ganja smoke. At first, I thought it came from the clothes that I had worn to the ganja-cutting expedition earlier in the day, but then I saw some young men smoking up.

I got on the bus and was soon rocked to sleep.

A Failed Raid in Koraput

It was nine 9.45 pm when we reached Koraput. I couldn't get a room at the Circuit House or in any of the hotels as all the rooms were full of tourists. Perhaps the hype around the Koraput Coffee Plantation was the reason, or maybe they were just fleeing the madding crowds of their breathless cities.

I finally managed a room in a training centre for government officers. The centre had no kitchen, so I had to ask one of the caretakers to get me some food from outside. I was sticky from the day-long ganja-cutting expedition and the evening bus ride, and I wanted a bath, but there was no hot water. This was December, and although the sun had been strong and hot in the Malkangiri forest, the Koraput night was cold. So, I had a choice: I could freeze and be clean, or I could sleep sticky. I chose the latter.

Before that, while I was waiting for the food, there was a call from the Excise Department, Koraput. The lady on the other side asked me to be ready by 6 am; a driver would pick me up from the training centre. I thanked her and settled down for dinner: a one-egg omelette, a few rotis and a potato-and-carrot curry. I was so hungry that the taste didn't matter. I wolfed it down, my hands still smelling of ganja. I was cold, so I asked the caretaker to get me some coffee. He obliged, but if I had thought I would get the much-hyped Koraput coffee, I was sadly mistaken. This was instant coffee. Ah, well. At least it was hot, and I went to bed warm.

I woke up around 5.30 in the morning all excited and put on the same clothes I had on during the Malkangiri expedition. I was ready to move before the driver arrived. I smoked an idle cigarette while drinking a cup of tea served by the caretaker of the training centre and looked out at the grey skeletons of buildings coming up on top of a hill.

Time passed; 6 am passed, and so did 7. Around 7.30, a driver finally called. 'Was I ready?' This time, a brand-new SUV drew up. I was quite surprised, but then the driver told me that one team had already set out, but a high-ranking officer of the Excise Department would be joining us, and I was to ride with him. So that explained the luxury. The driver switched on the heater to keep us warm, but it soon grew stuffy, and I asked him to turn it off.

We went to the high-ranking excise officer's house and waited a few minutes until he came out. I said hello and told him I could have gone with the other team. 'No room in those cars,' he said briefly. 'Full with junior staff.'

Forty kilometres later, we stopped at a police station where three or four more vehicles were waiting for us. When the officer got out of the car, many jawans saluted. Some thought I was an officer, too, and saluted me. I thought it only polite to respond in kind.

I had tea in a tea stall with the ganja-cutting team. They also bought water bottles, fruit and packets of puri and sabji or idlis for all of us to have in the field. Then, the party rolled out. With the police, it was now almost 40 men and women, with bush cutters and machetes in hand.

Twenty kilometres later, the vehicles reached a small hill. The party had received information about a huge ganja plantation along both sides of a canal, a few kilometres from the hill.

The ganja-cutting team had breakfast together, some sitting on the ground, some on huge stones and some standing. I was also offered idli and puri with aloo-mattar. Then, the search for the ganja plantation started with the team walking through a huge plantation of eucalyptus trees. The narrow pathways in between the plantation led to the canal. Then a lady constable shouted, 'Here, look! So many ganja leaves on the ground. Someone must have transported ganja along these roads just a while ago.'

The team followed the same tracks and, after two kilometres, arrived at fields on the banks of the canal filled with freshly cut ganja plants, their stems still oozing sap.

Obviously, someone had informed the farmers of the raid. I learned later that ganja destruction expeditions had already been cancelled twice over the last three days. The farmers had had enough time to harvest the 30-odd acres of near-ready plants.

There was information about more ganja fields on the other side of the canal. Some jawans waded through the muddy waters to the other side, carrying the bush cutters on their shoulders, while another party kept walking along the canal banks through all the freshly cut ganja, looking dejected at having missed a big catch.

After a trek of almost two kilometres, the search party found another patch of nearly an acre with very good quality mature ganja plants still standing. A farmer who was cutting the plants spotted the search party approaching and dashed off into the forest. A little distance away could be seen another patch of harvest-ready plants.

The team could only manage to destroy around two acres of ganja plantation.

Disappointed, the team leaders decided to head back to the vehicles and go to another spot.

While returning, I overheard some of the jawans talking amongst themselves about informants on both sides. Apparently, many people in the Excise Department also worked as informants for the ganja mafia.

One of the jawans said, 'In this part of Koraput, young people come from different states of the country to work for the drug mafia. Recently, a young man was arrested for smuggling ganja. Sometime later, the Rajasthan police came for him because they had traced bank transfers of more than Rs 50 lakhs between this guy and a drug mafia in Rajasthan.'

Just then, I saw two men on expensive bikes crossing us on the narrow path. They were probably keeping an eye on the ganja-cutting team's movements.

The jawan told me another story about a policeman who took voluntary retirement because he was being transferred out of the ganja plantation area. The cop said he had made enough to last more than a lifetime, but there was so much more to be made; he would lose all that if he got transferred.

What more would I learn?

Next stop: Rayagada.

In Rayagada

At the Koraput bus stop, I was told that all the seats on the bus to Rayagada had been booked, so I would have to travel the 110 kilometres standing.

The Odisha State Road Transport Corporation (OSRTC) bus was packed. There were already about 30 people standing in between the two rows of seats, but the bus conductor kept pushing all the passengers to the back until it was difficult to find any space to set your foot down, and once you had found those few inches, you did not dare to move a millimetre. I ended up at the back of the bus, and despite the crowds, such was the condition of the shock-absorbers of the bus that each time it went over a bump on the road, I flew up almost a foot and nearly hit the roof.

Two people seated next to me were chatting. I ignored them until I heard the word ganja...

One of them said, 'You know what? One of my next-door neighbours recently bought a car. And this after a few motorbikes last year.'

The other said, 'I know people in my village who earn so much money from ganja that they have not only tiled the floors of their homes, they have even tiled the walls.' He paused and then added: 'Sometimes, I feel like quitting this government clerk's job and starting my own ganja transportation business.'

The first man responded to this with a warning: 'This bad money from ganja comes easy and goes easy. And one day, it takes you behind bars.'

We reached Rayagada around ten in the night. The autorickshaw driver I found didn't know where the circuit house was but asked me for Rs 130 for the trip. I showed him the place on Google Maps and said it was only two kilometres away. But the driver still took a long, circular route to the circuit house and charged me more than Rs 250.

I waited for a room for almost 45 minutes outside until a high-ranking officer of the district called and apologized and said, 'You will get a room; someone will be there with you within five minutes. If you need anything else, please feel free to message me.'

I said I needed a bit of help setting up a meeting with someone from the Excise Department.

'I will ask someone to call you,' he said. I was not even done with the call when someone came running and took my luggage.

At the entrance were two prominent posters put up on the wall: ALCOHOL CONSUMPTION IS PROHIBITED HERE. But then I passed a man walking out, and he certainly smelled of alcohol. So did the man who was carrying my bags. I handed the latter man a 500-rupee note, asked him to get me some rice, dal and vegetables and a bottle of beer.

Before the food came, someone from the Excise Department called and reminded me that the next day was a Sunday and it was also Christmas Day, so he was on leave, and illegal ganja farm destruction was on hold for the next few days. But someone from the Excise Department would meet me in the morning to help me with the information I wanted.

The food came, and so did the beer, I was so hungry that I finished it all in ten minutes and, tired after standing for more than 100 kilometres in a packed bus, I hit the bed and went to sleep instantly.

The next morning, I was waiting for tea when someone called and said that he had come to meet me on instructions from the excise officer, and was waiting outside my room. I opened the door, and we greeted each other and I invited him in.

He told me of the many ways the drug peddlers transport ganja illegally. First, the ganja is wrapped in newspapers and then put inside polythene bags and then wrapped again securely with brown sellotape. Then, the packet is sprayed with chemicals to disguise the smell. Sometimes, the ganja is hidden inside paddy-dust packets to smuggle it from Rayagada to Andhra Pradesh. Potato and ginger harvests are also used to smuggle ganja. So is banana and turmeric; even scrap from various scrapyards is used to conceal and smuggle ganja.

Many local youths are recruited to carry ganja in big trolley bags to bigger cities on trains, travelling as job seekers. The mafia uses new guys all the time so that no one gets suspicious about a familiar face.

'We don't have a single sniffer dog, so it's almost impossible to know who is travelling with what,' the excise officer said. 'And you can't stop everyone on suspicion.'

He shook his head and had his tea silently after that.

~

Since the ganja destruction raid was on hold in Rayagada for the Christmas holiday, I decided to move to my next destination.

The kindly excise officer arranged a vehicle to take me to Paralakhemundi in Gajapati.

'You don't have to pay anything, sir,' he said when I asked. 'I'm sorry we couldn't help you much due to the holidays. If you stay here for a few more days, we could show you everything you want.'

I thanked him and got into the car.

Travel to Gajapati

On the road to Gajapati, we stopped at a small tea stall in a market. The driver asked for tea in Telugu, I asked for a cigarette and a dantkili (a locally made chakli) to have with the tea. On the verandah of a house right next to the stall was seated a woman with four or five gold chains around her neck—each chain so thick, I wouldn't have been surprised if it weighed half a kilo. She coughed to clear her throat, making the chains tremble, and said something to a boy standing next to a Bajaj M80 moped. I took out my mobile phone to click a picture.

'What are you photographing?' the woman asked.

'These mopeds are very rare now, I just want to click a picture,' I said.

'This is our family's oldest vehicle, and that's why we still have it; it is what made us rich,' she said proudly.

I wondered if the family had made its money from ganja smuggling as well. Then I was ashamed at my prejudice. Why couldn't it be just hard work in business?

Then something about this thought seemed wrong, too. Why couldn't transport of bhang and ganja be a respectable business? Tomorrow, if weed is legalized, it wouldn't be a crime. Already, it was perfectly legal in many countries, as it had been for centuries, even in ours.

I asked the tea seller where I might find a kilogram of ganja.

He didn't look surprised. He said: 'You can find smaller quantities in a nearby shop. But I'll have to ask about that much.'

Some other customers had heard our exchange. There was no reaction. It was as if I had asked for a kilo of rice or sugar.

I reached Paralakhemundi, the district headquarters of Gajapati, around five in the evening. The circuit house there is a repurposed maharaja's palace. When you enter it, the first thing you notice is the floor, covered with beautiful tiles with floral motifs, then a table tennis table of finely polished stone. These are as they were in the original palace. The rest of the building has been renovated.

I was assigned a room quickly, unlike in Rayagada, and since I had informed the senior officers of my arrival, two junior officers from the Excise Department came to meet me later in the evening.

Here, too, the Christmas holidays meant that the ganja plantation destruction expeditions were on hold and would only resume around 28 or 29 December. But the junior officers said they would be happy to talk to me or give me any information I wanted about the department and its work in the district.

They started talking about the lack of manpower in their department and how they still managed to do a good job with the few resources they had.

One of them spoke about the problems they had tackling drug peddlers who moved ganja within and outside the district.

'It becomes difficult because some corrupt police officers are also involved. They take bribes to give the drug peddlers safe passage across district borders and even state borders.'

All this information was given to me on condition of anonymity.

On one occasion, I was told, while the Excise Department was tracking the movements of vehicles in and out of the district, they saw two young men in a car with West Bengal license plates enter a small village in the night. The next morning, the same car had an Odisha number plate and was heading to the border on its way back. The Excise Department surveillance team stopped it and started interrogating the two young men. They team was sure that one of the men was a local who was helping the other–a man from West Bengal–navigate the roads and was also working as a go-between. They searched the vehicle for a long time but were unable to find anything in it. They kept up the pressure on the local man and finally offered him a deal. He would not be mentioned in the chargesheet if he told them where the ganja was hidden in the car. At this, he cracked and told them that the back seat of the car had a chamber made of iron. The team went back and checked the car again, and indeed, there was a chamber–with several kilos of ganja in it.

'We sometimes let the small guys carry on with their business and keep tabs on them so that we can get to the bigger drug peddlers,' the other excise officer said. 'We also use their rivalries to our advantage; they often give us information against each other.'

The discussion went on for a while. I had a beer in between and a few cigarettes. The excise officers told me that I could visit their office in the morning, and someone would come and pick me up and take me to their office to meet an opium addict, as I had requested.

~

The next morning, at the excise office, one of the junior officers showed me a seized vehicle and said, 'After we seized this last truck a couple of months ago, we have no space left to keep any more seized vehicles in our office compound. Even to make space for this big truck, we had to move many of the two-wheelers we'd seized to the rooftop. We also don't have much space left to store the seized bhang or ganja, and the process of destroying it takes time.'

The opium addict arrived, and I asked if there might be a translator since the man only spoke Telugu. Fortunately, there was one, and he was free.

The opium addict informed me that he worked as a goldsmith and had already taken his morning quota of half a gram of opium. His story was an interesting one, and I have recorded it earlier in the book, in the chapter 'The Opium-card Holding Goldsmith'.

When we were done with the interview, the goldsmith invited me to see his work and have tea with him. I asked if he could make a gold nose pin for my girlfriend before I caught my train back to

Bhubaneswar at around four in the evening.

'It won't take more than twenty minutes, sir,' he said.

Half an hour later, after a payment of Rs 1,600, I had a beautiful gold nose pin.

The circuit house caretaker took me to the railway station on his motorbike. On the way, he showed me the beautiful palace of the Parala Maharaja. The maharaja, one of the richest royals of Odisha, had built the railway station just behind his place and had a train for his personal use.

'All the colleges and schools and the hospital you see in the town today–they were all built by him,' the caretaker said.

Since the train back to Bhubaneswar was almost two hours late, the caretaker showed me around the station, especially the old platform, which had the same beautiful floral tiles I had seen in the table tennis room of the circuit house.

~

Back in Bhubaneswar, the papers and TV channels were full of sensational news about the deaths of two Russian tourists, one of whom was prominent critic of Vladimir Putin.

The New Indian Express of 27 December 2022 carried this report:

> **International spotlight after dead tourist in Odisha found to be Russian tycoon and Putin critic**
>
> *…His [Pavel Antov's] postmortem report pointed at rupture of [the] left side of lungs, liver and spleen, leading to haemorrhage, shock and death. [Vladimir] Bydanov's postmortem report found 100 ml fluid in the stomach with a 'peculiar smell, like opium or ganja, i.e., cannabis'. Viscera of both the friends have been sent for further tests.*
>
> *The Russian group was believed to have been travelling to this part of Odisha for tribal tourism. Districts such as Kandhamal, Rayagada and Koraput are home to primitive tribal groups which attract international tourists. Also, the region is known for its cannabis.*

Travel to Kandhamal

You can only take a bus to Phulbani, the district headquarters of Kandhamal; there is no train nor any other means of transport available from Bhubaneswar. But the ganja from Kandhamal is considered the best in Odisha; smokers say this is because the weather there is cold, and this has something to do with the potency of the ganja. (Interestingly–or not–turmeric from Kandhamal is also considered the best in Odisha and among the best in India.)

The state transport bus was scheduled to depart late afternoon, around 4.45. Since I was almost an hour early, I went looking for a government-licensed bhang shop I'd heard about. I'd been told it was in a lane next to the bus stop, but when I reached the spot, I found that it had been demolished, along with other structures there, for the construction of a new bus terminus. I asked around and was told that the seller now stands just outside the bus stand and sells bhang from a bag.

I looked. He didn't seem to be anywhere in sight.

'May have gone to have tea,' said another hawker and shrugged.

Back I went to the makeshift bus stop teeming with busy humanity, full of dust and garbage, reeking of piss and with no place to sit, as the city waited for the new 'world-class' bus terminal. The waiting hall of the state transport department had less than 20 chairs and no toilet or drinking water facility.

But at least we left on time. It would be a 200-kilometre journey of over five hours. I slept until the sound of a quarrel woke me. Outside, moonlit hills. Inside, a man and a woman fighting over how the man controls all the money and doesn't leave even a paisa with the woman. Then the agitated woman threw up, and the stink almost set me off, too. Then, the quarrel resumed.

I wondered how I would get through the next few hours, but at the next stop, the woman got off, her puke in a plastic bag. Things got less malodorous and noisy thereafter.

The bus stopped at a few more places, dropping off passengers and taking on more. People got down, the men pissed by the road, had tea and pakoras, smoked cigarettes, and we finally reached Phulbani around ten in the evening.

I got out of the warm bus into a cold evening, but personnel from the Excise Department were at the bus stand with a comfortable car to take me to the circuit house. We stopped at a small restaurant to pack a couple of naans and some vegetable curry for dinner.

At the circuit house, the caretaker asked who had sent me and then called someone on the phone to confirm. Perhaps he still wasn't entirely sure about me, for he then gave me the worst room available in the entire circuit house. I had to inform him that I knew the senior officers of the district, and that it was one of them who had asked his staff to book a room for me at the circuit house. That kind of thing always works, and it did this time, too. I was moved into a VIP room. (Each circuit house has at least three types of rooms: one for commoners, one for the VIPs and another for the VVIPs. Space permitting, some have a dormitory for the drivers and other security personnel who accompany the VIPs and VVIPs. This is the case across India, without exception.)

Perhaps the caretaker was embarrassed about his 'mistake', for he hung around as I had my dinner and tried to make conversation. He told me how the 'Burra Sahib' and 'Madam'–by which, I think, he meant the district collector–liked him very much.

'They came to stay here with their dog,' he said.

'I took utmost care of them. And the dog, sir, a Labrador, he fell in love with me. He began to love me more than Sir or Madam. They found this funny. They said I should go to their bungalow and see the dog sometimes. But where can I go, sir? How many times do I get to go? There is so much work here. But I did go once, yes, and the dog remembered! He was so happy to see me.'

A pause. Then: 'I didn't know who had sent you, sir, or I would have given you the best room, sir.'

'Can I have a cup of tea?' I asked.

'Would you like green tea, sir? We have green tea now. Everyone drinks green tea, sir.'

He tried to show me some photographs of himself with Sir and Madam and the Lab, but perhaps he was too drunk to navigate his phone, for he kept hissing and sniffing at the things that showed up as he swiped away madly.

The night was cold for me, and though I had a sheet and a blanket, I wasn't really warm. The morning started with an upset stomach, so I decided to skip breakfast and only had green tea and water to hydrate my body since I had a long day of walking ahead of me. I wanted a good hot shower, but the hot water was limited to the tap. This could not be a VIP room, I realised, but it was too late to make a fuss. I filled a bucket with hot water and took a bucket bath.

While waiting for the excise personnel, I saw a few puppies and two mother dogs playing with the circuit house caretaker. The cleaning lady told me she spent around Rs 30 on biscuits every day for the dogs.

At 8.15 am, an officer from the Excise Department arrived, and we set off for Gochhapada Police Station, about 45 minutes away. There, we were joined by a group of around 25 DVF jawans and 10 or 12 labourers and other Excise Department staff, along with a few police officers. This ganja-cutting party moved out in three jeeps and a minibus towards a small village named Kudali, covering first some 20 kilometres on pucca roads and then another ten on muddy roads. The caravan stopped at the end of the village near a school in an open field, where some of the team members unloaded rations from the bus to cook a meal while others unloaded the six bush-cutting machines. The school was chosen because it had a tube well and water was easily available.

Then, the ganja-cutting team started walking towards the hills on the outskirts of the village, topped and tailed by DVF jawans. After walking around two kilometres, the team came across a patch of one-and-a-half acres of almost ready-to-harvest ganja on a hill surrounded by trees.

This was only the beginning. More and more plots turned up on this and other hills, all created by clearing large patches of sal trees. The trees around each cleared patch had been left in place, perhaps as a camouflage.

The streams sometimes had submersible water pumps to bring in water; there were also subterranean electric wires. Some team members destroyed the water connections.

At one point, as a small patch of ganja plantation near a stream was being cut, a woman came running up and begged us to leave a few ganja plants so that she could at least recover her investment, which she said amounted to 5000 rupees. 'I have two children, sir,' she said with a smile. 'I have been farming ganja to give them a better life. Please leave some for this year; I won't do it again the next year. Last year, too, you destroyed all my ganja plants.'

I think the smile on her face was to soften the determined but already tired ganja-cutting party. It worked. The men did leave behind a few uncut ganja plants.

On another patch of land, there was potato, onion and radish. Next to it, in a hut under the shadow of a date palm, sat an old woman. A younger woman was cooking freshly cut radish with onion on firewood. I tried to strike up a conversation with her and offered her ten rupees for a radish, which she took with much hesitation. I thought about asking her whether she had heard of the government scheme of giving women gas cylinders, but I dropped the idea. She wasn't very communicative. We were intruders, after all.

When we got back to work, another old woman also begged us to leave her a few ganja plants. She told me they were Kondhs, and these hills had been their home for thousands of years. 'But we don't have any papers to prove it,' she said. 'The government wants papers. What papers does the land give? They drive us out of our land because they say we have no papers. Then we have to come to the forest.'

I asked for her name.

'Why should I tell you my name? Why should I trust you? You drive us into the forest, and then when we try to make a living, you come with your machines to destroy my farm. What has the government given us? Go on then, cut it all, destroy everything, then leave us alone and go away.'

Meanwhile, the labourers were working on the uprooted plants, selecting the best buds and nipping them off with scissors and putting them away in bags. The excise officer explained: 'The labourers get around three hundred and fifty rupees for this hard work.

But if they get some ganja, they can sell it in the local market and make decent money.' He sighed and added: 'This is probably the only reason we manage to get labourers to come and do this work. They don't like being cursed by the tribals.'

One of the labourers told me how 'ganja kali' (ganja buds) are made: 'Sir, first you choose the best buds from the plants. Once the leaves start yellowing, you hang them in the shade for a day or two. You have to shake them well so that the seeds and unwanted leaves fall off and then wrap them in a polythene bag and use long strings made of old cycle tubes to tie them well and tight and leave them for a day or two until the stickiness of the flowers binds itself. Once you untie the rubber tube from the wrapping, the ganja kali is ready.'

Meanwhile, the team walked further and found another ganja farm with a hut near it. The floor of the hut was covered with ganja seeds, and some ganja plants were hanging on a pole bar made of freshly cut branches. I also found a packet of plant bio-stimulant and soil conditioner; the label read: 'Recommended by SAUs/ICAR institutions, Ministry of Agriculture & Farmers Welfare, Government of India.'

It was close to noon. Some DVF jawans bathed in a stream while others stood guard. For the first time on this trip, I realised that the DVF jawans with us had no bullet-proof vests or helmets; they only had walkie-talkies and guns and bullets. Perhaps this was because they were not anticipating trouble.

By the time the team had managed to cut around 40 acres of ganja plants, it was 2.30 in the afternoon and time to head back to the base, near the school, where some of the team members had stayed back in the morning to cook food for all of us.

A 45-minute walk took us back to base, where we sat on the ground and ate rice, dal, chicken curry and salad off disposable plates. After eating, I tried to find a suitable place to throw away my used pharmocol plate when I saw a cow and a dog competing for the leftovers; eventually, they settled down to eat from the same plate. Two jawans took the big aluminium vessels in which the food had been cooked down to a nearby stream and washed them.

On the way back to Phulbani to catch a bus to my next destination, one of the Excise Department officials told me a story. One night, they were waiting–on the same road we were now travelling–to intercept a car suspected of smuggling ganja. They had blockaded the road, but the car didn't stop; it accelerated and slammed into the Excise Department vehicle. The men of the excise team were stunned; one of them was injured. Before they could recover from the shock and the whiplash, the suspect vehicle had vanished into the darkness.

On my way back to the bus stand, I saw young men in fine clothes and sunglasses drinking beer on the road next to a foreign liquor shop. It was an odd sight to see after my time in the forest and hills at the end of dusty, broken roads.

Travel to Boudh

I had decided to cover the 75 kilometres between Boudh and Phulbani by bus. I got a seat in the front row. Next to the driver on the gearbox (or engine cover) sat a girl in college uniform with a Playboy Bunny hairband. I wondered if she knew of the history of the club and the magazine. Probably not; she probably thought the bunny was cute or the colour suited her.

The bus lumbered along, making frequent stops to pick up and set people down as it made its way to Boudh. On the way, I was told that there was a district cultural festival on and most police personnel would be engaged in dealing with law and order and traffic management. So, the ganja-cutting expeditions were on hold for the next few days. But the helpful excise official accompanying me said I could visit the excise office to meet the officers there and talk to them.

I reached Boudh around seven in the evening. A friend's younger brother was at the bus stop to take me to the circuit house on his Bullet. He had brought a friend of his along, so we were three on a bike, none of us wearing helmets. We stopped the bike in front of the circuit house at a small stall for coffee. My friend's brother told me about his work: he was tasked with spreading awareness about health issues related to tobacco and other drugs. He felt my book might help people learn more about the bad effects of all drugs and stay away from them. I looked at the little kid inside the tea stall and asked him for a Gold Flake cigarette and lit up. My friend's brother did not seem to disapprove.

After finishing our coffee, we crossed the road and got to the circuit house. I was ushered into the best room I had had thus far, a VIP room, because this time, I was introduced as the brother of a big officer of the district. Dinner was also rather good: I was served rotis with santula (mixed vegetable curry without spices, a native dish of Odisha) and bhindi-aloo. I topped it off with a cup of tea. A good, warm shower to wash off the dust of a day's work in the ganja fields and the bus ride, and I was off to bed for a good night's sleep.

After breakfast—tea, upma with matar-aloo curry—the next morning, I walked to the old palace of the Boudh Maharaj. On the way, there was a troupe performing a dance on the road. I met my friends from the previous night, who told me that it was a street festival organised by the district administration in advance of the Boudh Festival and the Hockey World Cup, which was being hosted by the state for the second time. My friend's brother offered to take me to the palace on his Bullet. We looked around the old palace, which was almost in ruins, walked by the cinema hall, which had been shut for the last few years, and the old Buddha statue in a small temple in a park. Then the Excise Department called, asking me what time I would be coming to the office.

Fifteen minutes later, I arrived at the excise office where the big boss of the Excise Department met me. A junior staff member offered me a paper plate of cut fruit.

Although the ganja-cutting expeditions were on hold, the senior officer told me they could show me a plantation around 20 kilometres from the town. However, he said we must not go inside. And so, we set off in a jeep: two junior staff from the Excise Department, a driver, my friend's brother and me carrying two plates of cut fruit.

The excise staff sitting in the front passenger seat kept telling me stories of poverty in the area and how nobody was doing anything about it, how the local tribals were simple and were paying for being simple. According to him, the natives of Boudh lived on nothing. Though the tribals tended to the ganja farms, they did not make the money. The middlemen made the most profit, while the poor tribals always got arrested and went to jail.

After almost 45 minutes on the road and 20 minutes of walking, we ended up in a forest with no sign of ganja. All we could find were some wild berries, which I relished.

The older excise officer with us, however, wasn't going to give up; he suggested another spot, so we jumped into the jeep again and travelled for another 30 minutes or so. Then we crossed a small hilly patch and walked for around a kilometre and found a five-acre plantation of fully grown ganja. In the middle were two small huts. Inside, there were makeshift beds made of pieces of forest wood with a layer of paddy straw and blue plastic sheets. There were blankets and men's clothes lying around and smoke from a firewood chulha (earthen stove). I also saw huge quantities of ganja kali in used plastic cement bags wrapped with used bicycle tubes, all stocked and ready to be shipped.

There was no one around. The forest was quiet. The breeze whispered ganja songs through the plants, but I had the feeling we were being watched. I suggested it was time to move on since we had no police escort, and the excise officers also thought discretion was the better part of valour, and so we headed back to the jeep.

As we walked, we noticed a man come out of the forest and stand quietly, looking at our jeep. Then two sadhu-type men with long dreadlocks and just their lower bodies covered in orange gamchhas crossed our jeep on a bicycle, going towards the forest.

On the way back to the town, I was told about an incident that happened a few days back in Malkangiri when some policemen were thrashed by villagers for cutting down their ganja plants. One of the home guards was tied up and held hostage by the villagers until a larger group of policemen rescued him. This was the same area that I had visited a few weeks ago.

As our jeep took the road out of the forest, I called the officer in Malkangiri who had helped me and asked whether anyone from his team had been involved in that incident. Fortunately not, he said. It was another team that had been unlucky enough to get into that situation.

I felt very lucky that I hadn't been harmed on any of the trips. Even today, there had been only five of us, with no protection, in the ganja farms in Boudh, but we had managed to come out unharmed. As I was thinking this, I smelled ganja. Fresh ganja. I learnt later that one of the excise guys with us had got some for himself from the ganja field.

The excise men invited me to have lunch with them in their office, but I had already ordered lunch at the circuit house. I had fish curry, dal and rice with salad, paid Rs 680 to the circuit house caretaker towards my stay and food, signed in the register, rested for a while, and came to the bus stop to catch the 4.30 bus.

On the bus back to Bhubaneswar, everyone was talking about the Hockey World Cup. The chief minister had met the Bollywood actor Ranvir Singh and music composer Pritam at his residence, a man said. Another man said that the chief minister had asked everyone at the Hockey World Cup venue: '*Apanamaney khusi ta?*' (Are you all happy?)

What had the World Cup cost the state, I wondered. How many hundreds of crores? How many people had benefitted from the extravaganza?

Meanwhile, people in small villages had barely enough land to till and keep body and soul together. They planted ganja to make some money, and for this, they had to face the wrath of the state.

Back Where It Began

Puri in 2022

I never thought that the process of writing a book would mean coming back to Beach Road and spending a day or two doing the same shit I did for many years in the past.

I reached Puri in the afternoon. I went to see a friend named Deba, who was going to take me around. He warned me over cups of tea, 'Brother, the bhang scene has completely changed in Puri. All the bhang lassi shops have been forced to shut down. Now, you must drink bhang on the sly, and to make matters worse, we are not even getting good bhang these days.'

He went on: 'In our area, there is only one guy who comes to a coconut field near a pond every afternoon with bhang on his bicycle, and he is completely sold out in 30 minutes. We need to hurry, or we won't get our quota.'

We took along three one-litre plastic water bottles. We were joined by another guy named Gochi, a regular client of the bhang seller. When we reached the spot—in a patch of banana plants near the pond—the bhang seller hadn't yet arrived. But a client was waiting, and he assured us that the bhang was on its way.

Out of nowhere, six or seven others materialised, and we all waited together. The bhang seller finally rode up on a blue bicycle—a nondescript man in a green t-shirt, black shorts and green flip-flops, and with a colourful gamchha around his waist. Hanging from the handles of his bicycle were two repurposed cement sacks packed with used Bisleri PET bottles filled with a green liquid. That was the precious bhang, around forty litres of it.

The bhang seller quickly unloaded the cement bags, took out a couple of the bhang-filled bottles and a few stainless-steel drinking glasses and started serving us: a small glass of bhang for Rs 20 and a large glass for Rs 30. He did brisk business. The men gathered there gulped down the liquid bhang as if they had been thirsting for it for ages. Gochi had a huge smile on his face as he handed over three empty plastic water bottles to the seller. In between handing out glasses to the others, the bhang seller filled our bottles.

As soon as the bottles were filled, Gochi hid them in the bag he was carrying, and the three of us headed off to a hideout Gochi knew. As we drank the bhang,

Deba and Gochi kept complaining about how difficult it had become to get good ganja to smoke and how everything had changed in Puri. They showed me a packet of ganja they had got from the local bhang shop. It was still green, not completely dried yet. It seemed to me that someone had sourced freshly cut ganja from the Excise Department.

Deba and I left Gochi in his hideout and went to the excise office to meet the excise officer. The officer, who knew Deba, warmed up quickly and informed me that most of the bhang shops in Puri had shut down for lack of demand. 'Young people generally drink alcohol now, and brown sugar addiction is rampant,' he said. 'This is having a terrible effect on our young people. I think we should make bhang and ganja legal, so that people don't take the other drugs, which are not just harmful but also dangerous.'

Off the record, he also told us about a licensed bhang shop on Beach Road, which was shut down because the shop owner could no longer afford to give extortion money to the local mafia.

I said goodbye and headed to a hotel in the Beach Road area, where I had booked a room. It was three in the afternoon when I reached the hotel and stood at the deserted counter, waiting for the receptionist. He showed up ten minutes later and asked me to wait another ten minutes while he made some calls and struggled with the mouse and keypad of his desktop. Finally, he showed me my room. It didn't have an attached bathroom. But my booking on the travel portal had clearly mentioned a room with a terrace view and a private bathroom. When I asked the receptionist to give me a room with an attached bathroom as promised on the travel portal, he said the information on the travel portal was incorrect and I would have to pay another Rs 1,100 to get a room with an attached bathroom. I asked him to talk to his boss to resolve the issue. After much hesitation, the receptionist called up his boss.

I could hear the boss on the other end. He asked whether the guest was an Indian or a foreign national. On hearing that he was dealing with an Indian guest, the boss told the receptionist to inform me that they would not be able to do much about the matter and that I should get in touch with the travel portal or pay them the extra money to get a room with an attached bathroom.

I refused to give up. 'I want to speak to your boss,' I said, and the receptionist handed over the phone.

The owner of the hotel used to be a guy I had known well during my Beach Road years. But this man did not sound like him, so I kept to the issue at hand–I wanted the room that the travel portal had promised, and I would not pay anything extra. After a long discussion, the 'boss' agreed to give me a room with an attached bathroom.

I was still puzzled–who was this man I had spoken to? Was he a manager or really the owner of the hotel that I had spoken to? Yes, he was, the receptionist said. He told me this man had recently taken over the hotel on a lease from the original owner and boss.

I was relieved to hear this. So, my memory wasn't playing tricks on me after all.

The original boss of the hotel and I went back a long way...

I was around 19 when I first came to this hotel–let us call it Hotel X. I had come with a Norwegian group I had befriended on the beach. The six or seven men and women were on a long holiday and loved to smoke and drink. It was New Year's Eve, and they had asked me to join them in the celebration at their hotel.

It was late evening. We all gathered on the back veranda at a long table which could accommodate 25 to 30 people. From the veranda, stairs led down to a small sandy backyard filled with Australian pines; then, a tiny gate opened to the beach. The evening started with a lot of cheap Indian whiskey and lots of cigarettes, and then a lot of ganja. I was happy because all this was free for me. Then, more people joined us, a group of Indian men and women who spoke English and French and danced to Western music. It was lovely watching all those carefree people. The drinking and smoking continued.

At one point, while we were making joints on the table, a man threw a piece of something that looked like chocolate on the table and asked one of the foreigners to roll it. I asked my Norwegian friends about it, and someone said: 'Hashish.'

I had never heard of hashish, let alone had it. I watched in fascination as the piece of 'chocolate' was crushed and put in a chillum. The chillum was passed around. It gave off a smooth, sweet smell as we all took deep drags and got even higher and danced some more.

So, there we were; night and moon and stars and sea and hash. I was dancing, grooving, when, for the first time in my life, a woman came up to me and asked for the pleasure of a dance. We began to dance, and then more men joined in...Then came a huge shout, a bellow, from the guy who had given us the hash. He was pushing and slapping another man and ordering him to get out of the hotel. A waiter came running to me and advised me not to dance with the woman and to stay well away from her as the boss of the hotel was having a scene with her and he was crazy and might thrash me, too. There could be blood. There was a moment of silence as we all took in this news. Then, the woman was gone, and the music was thumping out again, and we began to move and groove. The party went on until midnight. We all hugged and wished each other Happy New Year and, finally, my Norwegian friends drifted off to their rooms.

I wandered out of the hotel and walked back home alone, drunk and smoking a joint.

I was telling this story to a friend the next day as we were smoking, and he said, 'You know who the boss of that hotel is, right?'

I didn't.

My friend cast me a where-do-you-live look and told me that the owner of Hotel X was the only son of a big-time political leader.

Just then, a constable walked up to me and asked me to come with him to the police van, which was parked on the other side of the road. I asked him why, but all he said was, 'Just come with me. Police Babu is calling you.'

When I reached the van, the 'Police Babu' said to me, 'Where do you get your ganja from? How dare you smoke it on the road? If I see you again on this road, I will put you behind bars.'

I said, 'I get bhang from the government bhang shop. It is perfectly legal.'

Police Babu snapped, 'Don't argue with me! I will break your legs if I see you smoking on the road again.'

Was this the fallout of that dance? I have never been able to tell.

Anyway, back to the present. I got my room with an attached bathroom, checked in, and went out to drink a few beers and see what had changed on Beach Road.

The first and most obvious visible change: no foreigners, only Indian tourists. And the road was writhing with hotels and restaurants. There was not an empty patch of land left on Beach Road.

I was expecting this, though the extent of the change shocked me.

Some of my friends who married foreigners have bought land and built hotels of their own and are looking to buy more properties. Some have moved to other countries, and some are still on the road, standing and smoking, looking for action. Always looking for action and paralyzed, looking and waiting for action. Life is passing them by.

I wandered down the road. Here's Sipu. Haven't seen him in years. He's still chill. But not all good, though.

Here's Papu. He was once a happy bhang drinker and ganja smoker. He married a Japanese and had a couple of kids with her–or was it more? They built a hotel together, Papu and his Japanese wife, and everything looked bright. Then he got hooked on brown sugar, and everything went down the tube. He lost the hotel. His wife left him and took the kids and went back to Japan. Now, he still smokes up and waits on the beach for a second chance at love and life.

One thing hasn't changed on Beach Road: the government bhang shop I used to frequent is still there, witnessing the ups and downs of the denizens of the area and visitors. But the old vibe is missing. There is a current of violence in the air. That happens when you're drunk, or you're mixing too many things.

~

I'm not sure I like this new Beach Road, this new Puri. To avoid the crowds, the tourists, Sipu, Deba and I get on my scooter and got to a small government-run bar a little distance away from Beach Road. Over beer, my Sipu says, 'I also want to write a book. It will be called "Forty-two Hours no Smoke no Fire".'

I'm not sure what this means. Maybe I misheard it, or maybe it is really deep. Maybe I should ask, but I don't. But we all cheer him on and say he should really write that book.

Sipu also keeps telling me how he has been

destroyed by people, and now, he has lost everything, but he is not finished, and, one day, everyone is going to pay for what they've done to him. He says the CIA, R&AW and Interpol are all part of the conspiracy to finish him off. I listened as he ranted on.

'They want to destroy me and my family.'

'They are following me; they are aways following me.'

I want to just hold him and soothe him and make him understand that it is time to quit ganja, bhang, booze and all the other drugs and substances that are fucking with his mind and turning him paranoid. I want to, but I just sit there, nodding like an idiot. Then I stop nodding. But he's still ranting on and on. I can see he isn't going to listen to reason. Reason is a stranger in Sipu-land. But tonight, reason is a stranger in my head, too. I'm losing it, too. It isn't Sipu alone who can't stop...

A few more beers and then back to Beach Road. Deba says we must check out a newly opened rooftop bar, and we do; we have a few more beers.

Then, go to the beach to look for a spot to drink some more and smoke some more.

We are smoking our way past a betelnut shop when someone asks Sipu, 'Hey, what are you looking at, you junkie?'

We are seconds away from a fight, so we decide to take it inside. Back on my scooter, back to Hotel X for more beer and food. We drink and smoke and talk and remember until the staff ask us to keep it down so that the other guests might sleep.

That starts Sipu off. '

'You saw that guy outside? You saw how he took me on? How he abused me? He wanted me to hit him. He wanted it because he was paid to do it. They are trying to destroy me. They have their spies. They send them around. They look at me, and when I look back, they attack me so that they can throw my ass in jail then and finish me off.'

We drink some more and then go out to the road and smoke joints. In the middle of the night. It's just like the old days.

I want to write when I get back to my room. But I'm drunk, I'm stoned, I can't write. I go to sleep, but I can't sleep. And then I can, and I wake up all hungover. I want juice, something clean and fresh and restoring, but the hotel doesn't have any, so I have a cup of coffee under the mango tree in the garden and then puri and sabzi for breakfast. I try to surface.

Next to me, a table full of young Indian men and a lone Italian. He looks at me, the Italian, and says, 'Group breakfast.' I realize that nothing has changed after all, and it is easy to get back to Puri, the Puri I lost ten years of my life in, but also the Puri where I was sometimes happy, sometimes wasted, the Puri where I met strangers for a day, a night; friends for a day, a night. I lived. A sort of life.

Puri. You carry your Puri with you, inside you, somewhere. Everyone has a Puri. I had my Puri—or it had me...

You smoke up, and the door opens, and you're on the threshold. Now you can walk in, you can just stay stoned, or you can turn away and walk away. Many tourists say: Puri paralyzes. People come here for a day or two and end up staying months without realizing how stoned they are.

I want to run away from Puri as soon as possible before I take up residence in the Puri of my past, the Puri of my heart, again.

~

Before heading back to Bhubaneswar, I wanted to have fish curry and see a few more government-licensed bhang shops. I went around the town looking for the bhang shops, but almost all were shut. One near the station was still open and was still selling ganja, though not openly. There was a licenced bhang shop on Grand

Road near Hospital Square. Interesting, because it was a mobile bhang shop on a little wooden cart.

Everything is now hush-hush about bhang and ganja, but brown sugar is easily available almost everywhere. I tried to look for the oldest bhang shop in Puri. It used to be near the temple, but people told me that when the government demolished the old buildings near the temple to start a heritage corridor, this bhang shop was also destroyed. Along with many old buildings of historical significance. The world moves on.

Tired, I had a beer with a complimentary boiled black gram in a dingy bar so dark in the middle of the afternoon that you could not see the guy sitting in front of you. Next: a great fish thali in a restaurant near the crematorium, Swarga Dwar. They say if you are cremated here, you go straight to heaven, hence the name. If you cross the road from the fish thali place, you can smell the burning bodies.

On our way back, we saw a guy in the middle of the road, high on something and challenging all passersby.

Deba said: 'Brown sugar playing its tricks on the poor fucker.'

Time to go back. Time to let the door close again. Time to go back to Bhubaneswar before I get caught in a cycle of smoking, drinking, sleeping, slumming, smoking, drinking, crying, sleeping, eating...

On the way back on my scooter, I kept seeing many advertisements for deaddiction centres and a new building with the signboard: 'Newlife Deaddiction Centre'.

I stopped at a tea shop on the highway to have a cup of tea and a smoke–just a cigarette–next to a canal by some paddy fields. There was a bunch of Patakapura bananas hanging from the roof of the tea shop on a coir rope.

I asked the guy if the bananas were ripe and ready to eat.

He said: 'These are pure desi bananas, sir, not like Singapore green bananas. Eat one, and you will know the difference, these are the indigenous bananas of this area. You won't find these in your cities.'

'I know,' I said. 'I was born in Puri.'

He said: 'Then you must know how good these bananas are. They won't make you cough, unlike other bananas.'

After having one or two sweet bananas, I asked for a cup of tea and a cigarette. While sipping my tea and puffing at my cigarette, I smelled the sweet smell of ganja. The tea seller was smoking a well-rolled joint. I asked him about the joint, and he took out a few cardboard boxes the size of candle boxes.

'Readymade joints. Available in many places,' he said.

The sleek black cardboard box read 'Dhur—premium pre-rolled cones'. It also said: 'Bomb size. Made with ultra-thin paper. Not for sale to minors.' And it had social media hashtags to follow.

Another box read: 'ATC Himalaya. Pre-rolled cones, bomb size, made with ultra-thin premium paper…MRP Rs 15/- (inclusive of all taxes)'

The tea seller said there were two types of readymade pre-rolled cone boxes, one type with ready-to-smoke ganja joints inside and another with empty pre-rolled joint cones. The first was for people who didn't want the bother of rolling, the second for those who had their own sources and wanted to roll their own.

The ready-to-smoke cones are Rs 35 each, the empty pre-rolled cones are Rs 10 each.

'There is a huge demand for these cones,' the tea seller said. 'Many engineering students, MBA students, law students—all the big college students smoke these. Even girls like these. The suppliers come to shops like mine, and somehow, people know, and then they come and ask for a cone.'

I was reminded of the days when getting cigarette paper was difficult. There were only two or three types of rolling paper available in the market: Capstan, Wills, and Charminar. They were all small-sized rolling papers, and very few people knew how to roll. Now, the demand is so high that someone has turned it into a retail business!

I bought a few of the pre-rolled ganja cones for my reference and said goodbye to the tea seller.

And then a moment of truth: a fear starts somewhere that the police might apprehend me and arrest me for possession of illegal drugs.

Then, some days later, just before I sent the manuscript off to my editor, something popped on my twitter feed:

> Bolangir | Farmers seek permission to grow ganja instead of paddy alleging lack of paddy procurement in mandis; they submit memorandum to district collector & threaten to commit suicide if denied permission. #Odisha
>
> Tweet from @otvnews

Acknowledgements

I don't know where to start, but thank you so much to the people who have believed in me at every step of my life and also those who haven't—all of whom motivated me to keep doing my thing and not stop.

Thanks to ganja and bhang, despite everything, for making me mad.

My dear friend and publisher Ravi, who kept pushing me to write and taking my long phone calls and listening to me for hours with patience.

Dear Jerry, for the valuable inputs and editing the first draft with great care and patience.

To my love and partner Satabdi, who has been there for me for the last ten years, though it can be tough, and still makes me tea and food and takes care of my health and makes sure I am alive.

Writer Harihar Panda, thank you for the beautiful chapter on bhang from your book.

Thank you to my mother, Kumudini, for giving me some money and gold to run away from home.

Thank you to the Excise Department of Odisha for all the support and for taking care of me on the field.

Thanks to the district administrations of Malkangiri, Koraput, Rayagada, Gajapati, Kandhamal and Boudh.

Thank you, dear friends Nikhil Pawan Kalyan and Ravishankar Shukla.

Special thanks to Dipu, Pecha and Beach Road, Puri.

Thank you, Louise, for believing that I could write a book one day.

Thank you, Paul and all the visitors to our shores, for teaching me languages and many more things in life.